EXPLORERS
IN THE
20TH AND 21ST
CENTURIES
FROM AUGUSTE PICCARD
TO JAMES CAMERON

EXPLORERS
IN THE
20TH AND 21ST
CENTURIES

FROM AUGUSTE PICCARD
TO JAMES CAMERON

EDITED BY KENNETH PLETCHER, SENIOR EDITOR, GEOGRAPHY

Britannica
Educational Publishing

IN ASSOCIATION WITH

ROSEN
EDUCATIONAL SERVICES

Published in 2014 by Britannica Educational Publishing
(a trademark of Encyclopædia Britannica, Inc.) in association with Rosen Educational Services, LLC
29 East 21st Street, New York, NY 10010.

Distributed exclusively by Rosen Educational Services.
For a listing of additional Britannica Educational Publishing titles, call toll free (800) 237-9932.

First Edition

Britannica Educational Publishing
J.E. Luebering: Director, Core Reference Group
Adam Augustyn: Assistant Manager, Core Reference Group
Marilyn L. Barton: Senior Coordinator, Production Control
Steven Bosco: Director, Editorial Technologies
Lisa S. Braucher: Senior Producer and Data Editor
Yvette Charboneau: Senior Copy Editor
Kathy Nakamura: Manager, Media Acquisition
Kenneth Pletcher: Senior Editor, Geography

Rosen Educational Services
Jeanne Nagle: Senior Editor
Nelson Sá: Art Director
Cindy Reiman: Photography Manager
Brian Garvey: Designer, Cover Design
Introduction by Richard Barrington

Library of Congress Cataloging-in-Publication Data

Explorers in the 20th and 21st centuries: from Auguste Piccard to James Cameron/edited by
Kenneth Pletcher.—First Edition
       pages cm—(The Britannica guide to explorers and adventurers)
"In association with Britannica Educational Publishing, Rosen Educational Services."
Includes bibliographical references and index.
ISBN 978-1-62275-022-1 (library binding)
1. Explorers—Biography—Juvenile literature. 2. Discoveries in geography—Juvenile
literature. I. Pletcher, Kenneth, editor. II. Title: Explorers in the twentieth and twenty-first
centuries.
G200.E884 2014
910.92′2—dc23

                                                                                            2013009313

Manufactured in the United States of America

On the cover: Three members of Team Hi-Tec, including Ranulph Fiennes *(far right)*, hike
across a glacier as part of the Discovery Channel's 1999 Eco Challenge in Patagonia. *Graham
Chadwick/Getty Images*

CONTENTS

2

8

22

118

128

131

159

166

174

INTRODUCTION

Mention the word explorer and the image that comes to mind might be one of the great sea captains sailing a wooden ship into uncharted waters to find new lands, or a rugged pioneer blazing a trail westward into the American wilderness. As much as these classic portraits of exploration endure, the exploits of modern explorers and adventurers has necessitated a few additions to the gallery of associated images. This book describes how some of the greatest adventures of the 20th and 21st centuries have refined the public's concept of exploration. The collected biographies herein help demonstrate how exploration continues to enhance humanity's understanding of Earth while building a measure of insight into the universe that lies beyond this planet.

By the turn of the 20th century, much of Earth's habitable regions had been explored and, in many cases, permanently settled. However, certain parts of the planet's surface remained something of a mystery, such as the North and South poles. Because of their remoteness and extreme climates, the Arctic and Antarctic regions posed a formidable challenge for explorers. In fact, because of the difficult conditions, a scarcity of landmarks to aid navigation, and the lack of wireless communication at the start of the 20th century, there is even some question as to who actually reached the North Pole first. Historically, the feat has been credited to Robert Peary of the United States, who claimed to have accomplished the feat it in 1909, though later study of Peary's expedition records have cast doubt on whether he actually got there at all.

The first visit to the South Pole was less controversial but was still a sensation, both then and now. In early 1912, a British expedition led by Robert Falcon Scott reached the South Pole, only to find evidence that Norwegian explorer Roald Amundsen had beaten them there by about a month. Scott and his remaining men died tragically on the way back, trapped by a blizzard only 11 (18 km) miles from a supply cache that probably would have allowed them to reach their final camp.

The futuristic Solo Spirit *soars high above Tahiti in 2001, with millionaire adventurer Steve Fossett aboard. Fossett piloted a similar balloon for the first solo flight around the world the following year.* AFP/Getty Images

Despite the disappointing result and fatal ending, the bravery of the attempt made Scott a national hero. This underscores perhaps one of the most important points about the races to the North and South poles. These endeavours captured the imagination of the public and created a great deal of excitement. Even as the unknown regions of the world were getting fewer, the public's appetite for adventure was never greater. Case in point was archaeologist Howard Carter's 1922 discovery of King Tutankhamen's tomb in Egypt. Fascination with all things Egyptian had existed since the 4th century BCE, with the movement experiencing pockets of resurging interest throughout the centuries. The Tutankhamen find sparked a frenzy of what became known as "Egyptomania" that lasted until the end of the World War II. Film, literature, architecture, and other visual arts of the period all were heavily influenced by the Egyptomania craze. In fact, Egyptian-themed design was one of the important influences on the Art Deco movement of the 1920s.

During the period of exploration after 1900, reaching a new frontier could allow a person to go beyond the societal restrictions of the time, succeeding purely by having skills suited to the job rather than being judged by social status, gender, or ethnicity or race. So it was that an African American man, Matthew Henson, accompanied Peary on his trek to the North Pole, and in the decades that followed, women such as Gertrude Bell and Freya Stark became renowned for their travel adventures and associated writings.

At times, exploration of the past and politics of the present would cross, as was the case with T.E. Lawrence, who became popularly known as Lawrence of Arabia. Originally drawn to the Middle East by its wealth of archaeological findings, Lawrence soon became embroiled in the affairs of the region. He met leading figures of the Arab world while helping to organize them as a British ally against Turkey, which was then allied with Germany during World War I. A self-proclaimed mastermind of the uprising against the Turks on the Arabian Peninsula, Lawrence proved to be quite adept at military strategy and guerrilla warfare. His efforts toward creating a unified Arab state were never realized, although he remained an advocate for Arab independence for years after the fighting had ceased.

Around the same time a new frontier of exploration was opening up as adventurers took to the skies. By the 1920s, the airplane, which had been invented in the first decade of the 20th century, had become a valuable tool for exploration, as well as a cultural symbol of adventure.

Roald Amundsen, leader of the first expedition to reach the South Pole, later became one of the first people to fly over the North Pole. His initial attempt, in an airplane, was unsuccessful, but Amundsen, accompanied by notable aviators Lincoln Ellsworth and Umberto Nobile, used a dirigible to accomplish the feat. American Richard E. Byrd is another explorer who integrated aviation into his expeditions, particularly as part of the first crew to fly over the South Pole. By the late 1920s, the airplane had been around for more than two decades, but it still had significant limitations. One of those limitations was the distance that could be flown without stopping: the instruments needed for night navigation had not yet been developed, the mechanical components of airplanes required frequent maintenance, and figuring out how to carry enough fuel for an extended flight was a challenge. However, the dangers and difficulties of aviation only increased public interest in it, and a $25,000 prize (the equivalent of over $300,000 in modern-day dollars) was offered for the first nonstop flight between New York and Paris. American Charles Lindberg, who had been a barnstorming stunt pilot and a flier for early airmail service, rose to the challenge; in May 1927 he flew solo for more than 33 hours over the Atlantic Ocean. In the process, he became a national hero and expanded the possibilities for air flight.

In 1932 another American, Amelia Earhart, crossed the Atlantic by plane in just under 15 hours—a record at the time, as well as a measure of how much aviation had improved in the five years since Lindberg's pioneering flight. Earhart continued to push the envelope, becoming the first person to fly from Hawaii to California. She and her navigator, Fred Noonan, disappeared while flying over the Pacific Ocean in 1937 during the course of another adventure—an attempt to fly around the world. Still, her celebrity and accomplishments further stoked public enthusiasm for aviation, and also helped demonstrate what women were capable of accomplishing.

While Lindberg and Earhart were making daring flights that carried them high over open seas, other explorers were focused on diving deep into ocean depths. During the 1930s, William Beebe and Auguste Piccard began developing deep-sea diving craft capable of withstanding enormous water pressure while delivering breathable air. With these craft, it became possible for humans to descend thousands of feet down into the ocean, a feat that opened up an entirely new frontier of exploration. Interestingly, Piccard demonstrated that he could succeed at exploring both extremes of the biosphere. In addition to his work on the deep-sea-diving bathyscaphe, Piccard was also a pioneer in balloon flight. He developed a pressurized cabin that allowed him and a fellow scientist to reach altitudes above 50,000 feet (15,200 metres), where they studied cosmic rays. The post–World War II era saw Frenchman Jacques Cousteau outfit a converted military ship for oceanographic research. Cousteau's scientific work was significant, but even more important was his role in bringing deep-sea exploration to the public eye. First through his documentary films and later through a long-running series on American television, he showed people underwater wonders of this planet that they had never before seen and thus helped renew the public's fascination with exploration.

Another frontier that captured the public's attention throughout the 20th century was exploration of the highest places on Earth. The biggest prize of all—literally and figuratively—was Mount Everest, the highest point on the planet, reaching 29,035 feet (8,850 metres) above sea level. By the 1920s, mountaineers were determined to conquer that summit. Among them was Englishman George Mallory, who made three attempts to conquer Everest, dying on the third try. Decades later, evidence of Mallory's final expedition was found as high up as 27,700 feet (8,440 metres) on the mountain; it remains unknown, however, if Mallory and his climbing companion reached the summit before perishing. When asked why anyone would want to climb Everest, Mallory helped define the modern spirit of exploration when he responded simply, "Because it's there."

The challenge of Everest would remain a powerful lure for climbers for decades to come. In 1953, Edmund Hillary of New Zealand, accompanied by Tibetan mountaineer Tenzing Norgay, reached the mountain's summit and returned back down safely. Despite the technical difficulty and physical danger of the climb, Everest remains the ultimate challenge by which mountaineers seek to test themselves to this day.

Once modern explorers had crossed between the poles, plumbed the oceans' depths, and scaled Earth's highest mountains, it was only natural that their gaze would turn toward challenges and adventures beyond this planet and out into the new frontier: the cosmos. The race into outer space, which began in the 1950s, was part of a larger Cold War competition between the Soviet Union and the United States. The Soviets took an early lead, launching, in 1957, the first satellite and, in 1961, sending the first human, Yury Gagarin, into space. Ultimately, however, the United States earned the greater victory, when, in July 1969, Americans Neil Armstrong and Buzz Aldrin became the first humans to set foot on the Moon. Their journey to the Moon and successful return to Earth in their Apollo 11 spacecraft was not just a remarkable achievement for the United States, but was a feat that captivated the imaginations of people around the world. It was a spectacular reminder of what human courage, ambition, and know-how could achieve—in short, a reminder of why great explorers have been celebrated through the centuries.

Not all space exploration ended so triumphantly. In 1967, during testing for the first Apollo mission, three American astronauts died in a fire that incinerated the inside of their capsule almost instantly. Even in the space age, a hard truth that had been proven by previous explorers such as Scott and Mallory (as well as many others before them) still remained—that sometimes the price of discovery is the life of the explorer. In recent years, the exploration of space has increasingly focused on destinations much farther than the Moon, to outer reaches with environments hostile to humans. Out of necessity for both cost and to safeguard human life, machines rather than humans have been sent on those missions.

Technology has not usurped the thrill of discovery completely, however. There are still men and women willing to take risks and push boundaries in the modern era.

Recent decades have seen several prominent figures who have earned the label "explorer" or "adventurer." Dian Fossey and Jane Goodall immersed themselves not simply in another culture, but entirely different species—mountain gorillas for Fossey; chimpanzees for Goodall. In the 1980s, entrepreneur Richard Branson and businessman Steve Fossett were as well-known for their adventures as they were for their business acumen and success. Branson set records in both power boats and hot air balloons. Fossett accompanied Branson on a failed attempt to circumnavigate the world by hot air balloon, but later became the first person to accomplish the same journey as a solo airplane pilot. In the 21st century, filmmaker James Cameron parlayed his fascination with deep-sea exploration—the subject of many of his documentaries and a narrative thread that framed his blockbuster movie *Titanic*—into the successful design and deployment of a submersible watercraft.

The profiles in this book demonstrate that the passion for discovery is a persistent theme throughout human history. Through their examples, it remains clear that this passion is alive and thriving today. Undoubtedly, there will always be those remarkable individuals who want to overcome the next hurdle and push the frontiers of human endurance and knowledge a bit farther.

ROBERT EDWIN PEARY

(b. May 6, 1856, Cresson, Pennsylvania,
U.S.—d. February 20, 1920, Washington, D.C.)

The American Arctic explorer Robert Edwin Peary is usually credited with leading the first expedition to reach the North Pole (1909).

Peary entered the U.S. Navy in 1881 and pursued a naval career until his retirement, with leaves of absence granted for Arctic exploration. In 1886, with his African American associate Matthew Henson, he traveled inland from Disko Bay over the Greenland ice sheet for 100 miles (161 km), reaching a point some 7,500 feet (2,290 metres) above sea level. In 1891 Peary returned to Greenland with seven companions, including his wife and Frederick A. Cook, who in 1909 would claim to have reached the North Pole before Peary. On this expedition Peary sledged 1,300 miles (2,100 km) to northeastern Greenland, discovered Independence Fjord, and found evidence of Greenland's being an island. He also studied the "Arctic Highlanders," an isolated Inuit (Eskimo) group who helped him greatly on later expeditions.

During his expedition of 1893–94 he again sledged to northeastern Greenland—this time in his first attempt to reach the North Pole. On summer trips in 1895 and 1896 he was mainly occupied in transporting masses of meteoric iron from Greenland to the United States. Between 1898 and 1902 he reconnoitred routes to the pole from

Etah, in Inglefield Land, northwestern Greenland, and from Fort Conger, Ellesmere Island, in the Canadian Northwest Territories. On a second attempt to reach the pole he was provided with a ship built to his specifications, the *Roosevelt*, which he sailed to Cape Sheridan, Ellesmere Island, in 1905. But the sledging season was unsuccessful owing to adverse weather and ice conditions, and his party reached only latitude 87°06' N. Peary returned to Ellesmere in 1908 for his third attempt and early the following March left Cape Columbia on his successful journey to the pole. On the last stage of the trek he was accompanied by Henson and four Eskimo. Peary and his companions purportedly reached the North Pole on April 6, 1909. Peary returned to civilization only to discover that his former colleague, Cook, was claiming to have reached the North Pole independently in April 1908. Cook's claim, though subsequently discredited, marred Peary's enjoyment of his triumph. In 1911 Peary retired from the navy with the rank of rear admiral. His published works include *Northward over the "Great Ice"* (1898), *The North Pole* (1910), and *Secrets of Polar Travel* (1917).

Peary's claim to have reached the North Pole was almost universally accepted, but in the 1980s the examination of his 1908–09 expedition diary and other newly released documents cast doubt on whether he had actually reached the pole. Through a combination of navigational mistakes and record-keeping errors, Peary may actually have advanced only to a point 30 to 60 miles (50 to 100 km) short of the pole. The truth has remained uncertain.

ERICH DAGOBERT VON DRYGALSKI

(b. February 9, 1865, Königsberg, Prussia [now
Kaliningrad, Russia]—d. January 10, 1949,
Munich, Germany)

The German geographer and glaciologist Erich Dagobert von Drygalski led an expedition to the Antarctic (1901–03) as part of an international program of exploration.

Sailing under the sponsorship of the German government, Drygalski's party landed on Antarctica at about longitude 90° E, in the area now known as Wilhelm II Coast. They became trapped in the pack ice and were forced to winter about 50 miles (80 km) east of Gaussberg, an ice-free volcanic peak that Drygalski named and that was a notable discovery. The results of the venture were published in 20 volumes of scientific reports, *Deutsche Südpolar-Expedition: 1901–1903* (1905–31; "German South Polar Expedition"). His general account of the trip, *Zum Kontinent des eisigen Südens* ("Concerning the Continent of the Icy South"), appeared in 1904.

From 1906 to 1934 he was professor of geography at the University of Munich. In 1910 he took part in the expedition of Ferdinand, Count von Zeppelin, to the Arctic island of Spitsbergen (in the Svalbard archipelago), north of Norway, where he studied the influence of glaciers on land features. With Fritz Machatschek he published a comprehensive textbook on glaciology, *Gletscherkunde* (1942; "Science of Glaciers").

SVEN ANDERS HEDIN

(b. February 19, 1865, Stockholm, Sweden—
d. November 26, 1952, Stockholm)

Sven Anders Hedin was a Swedish explorer who led through Central Asia a series of expeditions that resulted in important archaeological and geographical findings.

Travels in the Caucasus Mountains, Persia (present-day Iran), and Mesopotamia when he was 20 and an appointment as an interpreter for the Swedish-Norwegian mission to Nāser al-Dīn, shah of Iran (1890), marked the beginning of Hedin's life of exploration. In 1891 he visited Khorāsān (northeastern Persia) and Russian Turkistan, and between 1893 and 1898 he crossed Asia to Beijing by way of the Ural Mountains, the Pamirs ranges, and Lop Nor (Lop Lake), in western China. Following the Tarim River through western China, he explored the Gobi (desert) from 1899 to 1902. He was the first to explore the Trans-Himalaya mountain range of Tibet and to prepare a detailed map of the country (1905–08).

Hedin's pro-German sympathies during World War I cost him influential friends and the trust of the British Indian, Russian, and Chinese governments. He was able, however, to initiate and conduct the important Sino-Swedish expedition of 1927–33, which located 327 archaeological sites between Manchuria and Xinjiang (westernmost China) and disclosed an extensive Stone Age culture in present-day desert and steppe areas. Signs of Old Stone Age culture were found, and artifacts from later Stone Age periods evidenced a life dependent on hunting and fishing. Agricultural implements were discovered on the China-Mongolia borderland. In 1928 Hedin solved the puzzle of the changing basins of Lop Nor, which were related to the shifting lower course of the Tarim River. His many published works include *Through Asia* (1898), *Southern Tibet* (13 vol., 1917–22), *My Life as an Explorer* (1926), and *The Silk Road* (1938).

FREDERICK ALBERT COOK

(b. June 10, 1865, Hortonville, New York, U.S.—d. August 5, 1940, New Rochelle, New York)

Frederick Albert Cook was an American physician and explorer whose claim that he had discovered the North Pole in 1908 made him a controversial figure. His fellow American explorer Robert E. Peary, who is generally credited with having achieved this feat in 1909, denounced Cook's claim.

Cook began practicing medicine after graduating from New York University in 1890. He soon achieved fame as an explorer, serving as surgeon on Peary's first Arctic expedition (1891–92) and leading others to explore and climb Mt. McKinley (1903–06). Cook's claim that he had reached the North Pole on an expedition in 1908 was immediately disputed by Peary. Cook's Inuit (Eskimo) companions on his journey later asserted that he had stopped short hundreds of miles south of the Pole, and that the photographs of his expedition were actually shot at locations far distant from the North Pole. The controversy between Cook and Peary lasted until World War I, after which time public support for Cook's claim disappeared. Cook was later charged with fraudulent use of the mails and imprisoned in 1923. He was paroled in 1930 and given a presidential pardon in 1940.

MATTHEW ALEXANDER HENSON

(b. August 8, 1866, Charles county, Maryland, U.S.—d. March 9, 1955, New York, New York)

Matthew Alexander Henson was the African American explorer who accompanied Robert E. Peary on most of his expeditions, including that to the North Pole in 1909.

Orphaned as a youth, Henson went to sea at the age of 12 as a cabin boy on the sailing ship *Katie Hines*. Later, while working in a store in Washington, D.C., he met Peary, who hired him as a valet for his next expedition to Nicaragua (1888). Peary, impressed with Henson's ability and resourcefulness, employed him as an attendant on his seven subsequent expeditions to the Arctic (1891–92; 1893–95; 1896; 1897; 1898–1902; 1905–06; 1908–09). In 1909 Peary and Henson, accompanied by four Inuit (Eskimos), became the first men to reach the North Pole, the rest of the crew having turned back earlier. Henson's account of the journey, *A Negro Explorer at the North Pole*, appeared in 1912. The following year, by order of President

Matthew Alexander Henson, African American explorer dressed for one of several Arctic expeditions he undertook with Robert E. Peary. Library of Congress Prints and Photographs Division

William Howard Taft, Henson was appointed a clerk in the U.S. Customs House in New York City, a post he held until his retirement in 1936. Henson received the Congressional medal awarded all members of the Peary expedition (1944).

JEAN-BAPTISTE-ÉTIENNE-AUGUSTE CHARCOT

(b. July 15, 1867, Neuilly-sur-Seine, France—
d. c. September 16, 1936, at sea off Iceland)

The French explorer and oceanographer Jean-Baptiste-Étienne-Auguste Charcot carried out extensive charting in the region of the Antarctic Peninsula.

The son of the distinguished neurologist Jean-Martin Charcot, the young Charcot himself studied medicine and worked at the Hospital of Paris from 1890 to 1894, when he was also connected with the Pasteur Institute. He served as chief of the clinic of the faculty of medicine at the University of Paris from 1896 to 1898. Within a few years he turned to exploration.

On his first Antarctic expedition (1903–05) he charted parts of the Palmer Archipelago, explored the Gerlache Strait, and sailed as far as the northern end of Adelaide Island. On his second expedition (1908–10) he charted the coast to Alexander Island and discovered Fallières Coast and the island that bears his name. Deception Island and Adelaide Island were charted in detail. In 1912 he published a two-volume report of his findings, *Autour du pôle sud* ("Around the South Pole").

On subsequent ventures, between 1921 and 1936, with a corps of specialists, he studied plankton in the English Channel and in the North Atlantic and made oceanographic studies around the Hebrides, in Arctic waters, and off the east coast of Greenland. On September 16, 1936, his ship was wrecked off Iceland. Only one man survived; Charcot and more than 30 others were drowned.

ROBERT FALCON SCOTT

(b. June 6, 1868, Devonport, Devon,
England—d. c. March 29, 1912, Antarctica)

British naval officer and explorer Robert Falcon Scott led the famed ill-fated second expedition to reach the South Pole (1910–12). Scott joined the Royal Navy in 1880 and by 1897 had become a first lieutenant. While commanding an Antarctic expedition on the HMS *Discovery* (1901–04), he proved to be a competent scientific investigator and leader and was promoted to captain upon his return to England.

In June 1910 Scott embarked on a second Antarctic expedition. Its aims were to study the Ross Sea area and reach the South Pole. Equipped with motor sledges, ponies, and dogs, he and 11 others started overland for the pole from Cape Evans on October 24, 1911. The motors soon broke down; the ponies had to be shot before reaching latitude 83°30' S; and from there the dog teams were sent back. On December 10 the party began to ascend Beardmore Glacier with three man-hauled sledges. By

Camp of the Scott polar expedition in Antarctica, c. 1912.
Library of Congress, Washington, D.C.

December 31 seven men had been returned to the base. The remaining polar party—Scott, E.A. Wilson, H.R. Bowers, L.E.G. Oates, and Edgar Evans—reached the pole on January 17, 1912. Exhausted by their trek, they were bitterly disappointed to find evidence that the Norwegian explorer Roald Amundsen had preceded them to the pole by about a month.

The weather on the return journey was exceptionally bad. Evans died at Beardmore (February 17). Food and fuel supplies were low. At the end of his strength and hoping to aid his companions by his own disappearance, Oates crawled out into a blizzard on March 17, at 79°50' S. The three survivors struggled on for another 10 miles (16 km) but then were bound to their tent by another blizzard that lasted for nine days. With quiet fortitude they awaited their death—only 11 miles (18 km) from their destination. On March 29 Scott wrote the final entry in his diary:

> *Every day we have been ready to start for our depot 11 miles away but outside the door of the tent it remains a scene of whirling drift.... We shall stick it out to the end, but we are getting weaker, of course, and the end cannot be far. It seems a pity, but I do not think I can write more.*

On November 12, 1912, searchers found the tent with the frozen bodies, geological specimens from Beardmore, and Scott's records and diaries, which gave a full account of the journey. After his death Scott was regarded as a national hero for his courage and patriotism, and his widow was given the knighthood that would have been conferred on her husband had he lived.

GERTRUDE BELL

(b. July 14, 1868, Washington Hall, Durham, England—d. July 12, 1926, Baghdad, Iraq)

Gertrude Margaret Lowthian Bell was an English traveler, administrator in Arabia, and writer who played a principal part in the establishment in Baghdad of the Hāshimite dynasty.

Bell's brilliant career at the University of Oxford, where she took a first in history in 1887, was followed by

Gertrude Bell (right), conferring with British diplomat Sir Percy Cox (middle) and an Arab leader in Mesopotamia during the first half of the 20th century. Mansell/Time & Life Pictures/Getty Images

some time spent in Tehrān, where her uncle Sir Frank Lascelles was British minister. Returning to the political and intellectual salons in England and Europe for a decade, she did not until 1899 embark on the career of activities on the Arabian Peninsula that made her famous. She visited Palestine and Syria in that year and was often back in the Middle East during the next decade, extending her travels to Asia Minor (present-day Turkey). Her heart, however, was set on an Arabian journey, which she began in 1913. She was only the second woman (after Lady Anne Blunt) to visit Ha'il, where she was not favourably received, although she ever afterward favoured the Ibn Rashīd dynasty in its struggle against the Ibn Sa'ūd dynasty. She never wrote a full account of this journey, though her literary output during the 20 years preceding World War I had been considerable, including *Safar Nameh*

(1894), *Poems from the Divan of Hafiz* (1897), *The Desert and the Sown* (1907), *The Thousand and One Churches* (1909), and *Amurath to Amurath* (1911). Her vast correspondence was published in an edited form in two volumes by her stepmother in 1927.

Perhaps her greatest work was a masterly official report on the administration of Mesopotamia during the difficult period between the end of World War I in 1918 and the Iraq rebellion in 1920. After a short period of war work in England and France, she plunged into the rough-and-tumble of Middle East politics, mainly in Mesopotamia, where she served in turn under Sir Percy Cox and Sir Arnold Wilson. She helped place the Hāshimite ruler Fayṣal I on the throne of Iraq in 1921. The last three years of her life were devoted to the creation of an archaeological museum in Baghdad. She insisted, for the first time, that antiquities excavated should stay in the country of their origin, thereby ensuring that the National Museum of Iraq, which is her monument in the land she loved, would possess a splendid collection of Iraq's own antiquities. Facing ill health and profound loneliness, Bell took a fatal dose of sleeping pills and died July 12, 1926, in Baghdad.

OTTO NORDENSKJÖLD

(b. December 6, 1869, Småland, Sweden—
d. June 2, 1928, Gothenburg)

The Swedish geographer and explorer Nils Otto Gustaf Nordenskjöld led an expedition to the

Antarctic that was distinguished by the volume of its scientific findings.

A nephew of the scientist-explorer Adolf Erik Nordenskiöld, Nils became a lecturer in mineralogy and geology at the University of Uppsala, Sweden, in 1894 and led a geologic expedition to southern South America (1895–97). His findings in Patagonia and Tierra del Fuego formed an important contribution to world glacial geology. On October 16, 1901, he sailed aboard the *Antarctic* from Gothenburg and the following February established an Antarctic station on Snow Hill Island off Graham Coast, where he wintered with five companions. Their ship, which had wintered at the island of South Georgia, latitude 54° S and due east of Tierra del Fuego, was crushed in the pack ice when it returned to relieve them in February 1903. Nordenskjöld's party was again forced to winter in the Antarctic until rescued by the Argentine vessel *Uruguay* in November 1903.

Nordenskjöld published his extensive findings in *Wissenschaftliche Ergebnisse der schwedischen Südpolarexpedition 1901–1903* (1905–20; "Scientific Results of the Swedish South Polar Expedition 1901–1903"). He subsequently became professor of geography (1905) and first rector of advanced commercial studies (1923) at the University of Gothenburg.

ROALD AMUNDSEN

(b. July 16, 1872, Borge, near Oslo, Norway—
d. June 18, 1928?, Arctic Ocean)

The renowned Norwegian explorer Roald Engelbregt Gravning Amundsen was the first to reach the South Pole, the first to make a ship voyage through the Northwest Passage, and one of the first to cross the Arctic by air. He was one of the greatest figures in the field of polar exploration.

Amundsen studied medicine for a while and then took to the sea. In 1897 he sailed as first mate on the *Belgica* in a Belgian expedition that was the first to winter in the Antarctic. In 1903, with a crew of six on his 47-ton sloop *Gjöa*, Amundsen began his mission to sail through the Northwest Passage and around the northern Canadian coast. He reached Cape Colborne (in present-day Nunavut, Canada) in August 1905, completing his transit of the passage proper, before ice halted his westerly progress for the winter at Herschel Island in the Yukon the following month. Amundsen and his crew resumed the journey in August 1906 and were greeted with a heroes' welcome when the expedition concluded in Nome, Alaska, later that month. This achievement whetted his appetite for the spectacular in polar exploration.

Amundsen's next plan, to drift across the North Pole in Fridtjof Nansen's old ship, the *Fram*, was affected by the news that the American explorer Robert E. Peary had reached the North Pole in April 1909, but he continued his preparations. When Amundsen left Norway in June 1910 no one but his brother knew that he was heading for the South Pole instead of the North. He sailed the *Fram* directly from the Madeira Islands to the Bay of Whales, Antarctica, along the Ross Sea. The base he set up there was 60 miles (100 km) closer to the pole than the Antarctic base of the British explorer Robert Falcon Scott, who was heading a rival expedition with the same goal. An experienced polar traveler, Amundsen prepared carefully for the

Roald Amudsen (right) *after planting the Norwegian flag in the frozen tundra of the South Pole.* Imagno/Hulton Archive/Getty Images

coming journey, making a preliminary trip to deposit food supplies along the first part of his route to the pole and back. To transport his supplies, he used sled dogs, while Scott depended on motorized sledges and Siberian ponies, both of which soon failed.

Amundsen set out with 4 companions, 52 dogs, and 4 sledges on October 19, 1911, and, after encountering good weather, arrived at the South Pole on December 14. The explorers recorded scientific data at the pole before beginning the return journey on December 17, and they safely reached their base at the Bay of Whales on January 25, 1912. Scott, in the meantime, had reached the South Pole on January 17, but on a difficult return journey he and all his men perished.

With funds resulting from his Antarctic adventure, Amundsen established a successful shipping business. He acquired a new ship, the *Maud*, and tried in 1918 to complete his old plan of drifting across the North Pole, but he was forced to abandon this scheme in favour of trying to reach the North Pole by airplane. In a flight (1925) with the American explorer Lincoln Ellsworth he arrived to within 150 miles (250 km) of the pole. In 1926, with Ellsworth and the Italian aeronautical engineer Umberto Nobile, he passed over the North Pole in a dirigible, crossing from Spitsbergen (in the Svalbard archipelago), north of Norway, to Alaska. Disputes over the credit for the flight embittered his final years. In 1928 Amundsen lost his life in flying to rescue Nobile from a dirigible crash near Spitsbergen. Amundsen's books include *The South Pole* (1912) and, with Ellsworth, *First Crossing of the Polar Sea* (1927).

LUIGI AMEDEO GIUSEPPE MARIA FERDINANDO FRANCESCO, DUKE (DUCA) D'ABRUZZI

(b. January 29, 1873, Madrid, Spain—d. March 18, 1933, Abruzzi City, near Mogadiscio, Italian Somaliland [now Mogadishu, Somalia])

Luigi Amedeo Giuseppe Maria Ferdinando Francesco, Duke d'Abruzzi. Library of Congress, Washington, D.C.

Luigi Amedeo Giuseppe Maria Ferdinando Francesco, Duke (duca) d'Abruzzi was a Spanish mountaineer and explorer whose ventures ranged from Africa to the Arctic.

The son of King Amadeus of Spain (who was also the Duke d'Aosta in Italy), Abruzzi was the first to ascend Mount St. Elias in Alaska (1897). His 1899 Arctic expedition reached latitude 86°34' N—a record for the time. In 1906 he was the first to scale the highest summits of the Ruwenzori Range in east-central Africa. His expedition investigated the geology, topography, and glaciology of the range; it mapped the range and named its major peaks, passes, and glaciers. In 1909 Abruzzi climbed the world's second highest mountain, K2, in the Himalayas, to a height of more than 20,000 feet (6,000 metres). During World War I he held a naval command in the Adriatic until 1917. He was later involved in exploration and colonization in Italian Somaliland.

HOWARD CARTER

(b. May 9, 1873, Swaffham, Norfolk,
England—d. March 2, 1939, London)

The British archaeologist Howard Carter made one of the richest and most celebrated contributions to Egyptology: the discovery (1922) of the largely intact tomb of King Tutankhamen.

At age 17 Carter joined the British-sponsored archaeological survey of Egypt. He made drawings (1893–99) of

Howard Carter. Encyclopædia Britannica, Inc.

Tutankhamen, gold funerary mask found in the king's tomb, 14th century BCE; in the Egyptian Museum, Cairo. © Lee Boltin

the sculptures and inscriptions at the terraced temple of Queen Hatshepsut in ancient Thebes. He next served as inspector general of the Egyptian antiquities department. While supervising excavations in the Valley of the Tombs of the Kings in 1902, he discovered the tombs of Hatshepsut and Thutmose IV.

About 1907 he began his association with the 5th earl of Carnarvon, a collector of antiquities who had sought out Carter to supervise excavations in the valley. On November 4, 1922, Carter found the first sign of what proved to be Tutankhamen's tomb, but it was not until November 26 that a second sealed doorway was reached, behind which were the treasures. Carter's diary captured the drama of the moment. After making a tiny hole in the doorway, Carter, with candle in hand, peered into the tomb.

It was sometime before one could see, the hot air escaping caused the candle to flicker, but as soon as one's eyes became accustomed to the glimmer of light the interior of the chamber gradually loomed before one, with its strange and wonderful medley of extraordinary and beautiful objects heaped upon one another.

For the next 10 years Carter supervised the removal of its contents, most of which are now housed in the Egyptian Museum in Cairo. He published *Thoutmôsis IV* (1904) and *The Tomb of Tut-ankh-Amen* (1923–33) with, respectively, P.E. Newberry and A.C. Mace.

Sir Ernest Henry Shackleton

(b. February 15, 1874, Kilkea, County Kildare, Ireland—d. January 5, 1922, Grytviken, South Georgia)

The Anglo-Irish Antarctic explorer Sir Ernest Henry Shackleton became famous for his attempt to reach the South Pole and his dramatic, remarkable journey back to safety.

Educated at Dulwich College (1887–90), Shackleton entered the mercantile marine service in 1890 and became a sublieutenant in the Royal Naval Reserve in 1901. He joined Captain Robert Falcon Scott's British National Antarctic Expedition (1901–04) aboard the ship *Discovery* as third lieutenant and took part, with Scott and Edward Wilson, in the sledge journey over the Ross Ice Shelf when latitude 82°16'33" S was reached. His health suffered, and he was invalided out on the supply ship *Morning* in March 1903. In January 1908 he returned to Antarctica as leader

of the British Antarctic Expedition (1907–09) aboard the *Nimrod*. The expedition, prevented by ice from reaching the intended base site in Edward VII Peninsula, wintered on Ross Island, McMurdo Sound. A sledging party, led by Shackleton, reached within 97 nautical miles (112 statute miles or 180 km) of the South Pole, and another, under T.W. Edgeworth David, reached the area of the south magnetic pole. Victoria Land plateau was claimed for the British crown during the expedition. On his return Shackleton was knighted and was made a Commander of the Royal Victorian Order.

In March 1914 the British Imperial Trans-Antarctic Expedition (1914–16) left England under Shackleton's leadership. He planned to cross Antarctica from a base on the Weddell Sea to McMurdo Sound, via the South Pole, but the expedition ship *Endurance* was beset off Caird coast and drifted for 10 months before being crushed in the pack ice. The members of the expedition then drifted on ice floes for another five months and finally escaped in boats to Elephant Island in the South Shetland Islands. Shackleton and five others sailed 800 miles (1,300 km) to South Georgia in a whale boat and then made the first crossing of the island, to seek aid. He led four relief expeditions before succeeding in rescuing his men from Elephant Island. A supporting party, the Ross Sea party led by A.E. Mackintosh, sailed in *Aurora* and laid depots as far as latitude 83°30' S for the use of the Trans-Antarctic party; three of this party died on the return journey.

Shackleton died at Grytviken, South Georgia, at the outset of the Shackleton-Rowett Antarctic Expedition; his exertions in raising funds to finance his expeditions and the immense strain of the expeditions themselves wore out his strength. Shackleton's publications are *The Heart of the Antarctic* (1909) and *South* (1919), the latter an account of the Trans-Antarctic Expedition.

HIRAM BINGHAM

(b. November 19, 1875, Honolulu, Hawaii—
d. June 6, 1956, Washington, D.C., U.S.)

Hiram Bingham was an American archaeologist and politician who in 1911 initiated the scientific study of Machu Picchu, an ancient Inca site in a remote part of the Peruvian Andes. Bingham may have been preceded by the German adventurer Augusto Berns, who, some schol-ars believe, visited the site in 1867. Whether or not he was preceded by Berns, however, Bingham and his work were the key catalysts for the archaeological investigation of sites in the Andes and other parts of South America.

As a boy, Bingham learned mountaineering from his father, a well-known Pacific missionary. This skill vastly aided his Inca research. In 1906, seeking to enhance his ability to teach Latin American history, he traveled the Andean route taken in 1819 by Simón Bolívar from Venezuela to Colombia. In 1908 he followed the old Spanish trade route through the Andes from Buenos Aires, Argentina, to Lima, Peru.

Bingham was a member of the history faculty at Yale University from 1909 until 1924. In July 1911 he directed a Yale archaeological expedition whose main objective was to find Vilcabamba (Vilcapampa), which was the "lost city of the Incas," the secret mountain stronghold used during the 16th-century rebellion against Spanish rule. Prospects for locating it were poor: not even the Spanish conquistadores had discovered it. Clues from early chronicles of the Incas were scanty. It was believed to be situated somewhere near Cuzco, Peru, where the problems of crossing the Andes were formidable. The expedition owed its success largely to Bingham's steadfastness and courage. He visited several Inca sites, sometimes risking his life to do so.

After arriving in Cuzco, Bingham was urged by the prefect of Apurímac, J.J. Nuñez, to search the vicin-ity of the Urubamba River valley for the fabled ruins of Choquequirau ("Cradle of Gold"), and Bingham suspected that site might be Vilcabamba. On July 24 Bingham was led by a Quechua-speaking resident, Melchor Arteaga, to the ruins of Machu Picchu. There he found well-preserved stonework remains and was particularly struck by the sim-ilarity of one of the structures to the Temple of the Sun at

Cuzco. In 1912 Bingham led the expedition that excavated Machu Picchu, and he returned there in 1915. He became convinced that Machu Picchu was Vilcabamba, and it was not until the mid-20th century that his claim was seriously disputed. Bingham's additional work in the region revealed the important sites of Vitcos and Espíritu Pampa, a larger ruin that was thoroughly excavated in 1964 by the American archaeologist Gene Savoy, who demonstrated it to be a more likely site for Vilcabamba. Bingham's publications on South America include *Inca Land* (1922), *Machu Picchu, a Citadel of the Incas* (1930), and *Lost City of the Incas* (1948).

Bingham entered politics and was elected lieutenant governor of Connecticut (1922–24). After winning the governorship in 1924, he almost immediately resigned to fill a vacancy in the U.S. Senate. He was reelected to a full term in 1926, after which he devoted himself to business interests. In 1951 he was appointed to the Civil Service Loyalty Review Board by President Harry S. Truman and helped investigate controversial cases of suspected subversion in the U.S. State Department.

WILLIAM BEEBE

(b. July 29, 1877, Brooklyn, New York, U.S.—
d. June 4, 1962, Simla Research Station, near
Arima, Trinidad)

The American biologist, explorer, and writer on natural history Charles William Beebe combined careful

William Beebe (left) *and John T. Vann with Beebe's bathy-sphere, 1934*. Encyclopædia Britannica, Inc.

biological research with a rare literary skill. He was the coinventor of the bathysphere.

Beebe was curator of ornithology at the New York Zoological Gardens from 1899 and director of the department of tropical research of the New York Zoological Society from 1919. He led numerous scientific expeditions abroad and in 1934 with Otis Barton descended in his bathysphere to a then record depth of 3,028 feet (923 metres) in the waters of the Atlantic Ocean near Bermuda. A noted lecturer, he received numerous prizes and honours for scientific research and for his books, both technical and popular. His books include *Jungle Days* (1925), *Pheasants, Their Lives and Homes* (1926), *Beneath Tropic Seas* (1928), *Half Mile Down* (1934), *High Jungle* (1949), *The Edge of the Jungle* (1950), and *Unseen Life of New York* (1953).

VILHJALMUR STEFANSSON

(b. November 3, 1879, Arnes, Manitoba,
Canada—d. August 26, 1962, Hanover, New
Hampshire, U.S.)

Vilhjalmur Stefansson was a Canadian-born American explorer and ethnologist who spent five consecutive record-making years exploring vast areas of the Canadian Arctic after adapting himself to the Inuit (Eskimo) way of life.

Of Icelandic descent, Stefansson lived for a year among the Inuit in 1906–07, acquiring an intimate knowledge of their language and culture and forming the belief that Europeans could "live off the land" in the Arctic by adopting Inuit ways. From 1908 to 1912, he and the Canadian zoologist Rudolph M. Anderson carried out ethnographical and zoological studies among the Mackenzie and Copper Inuit of Coronation Gulf, in Canada's Northwest Territories (now in Nunavut).

Between 1913 and 1918 Stefansson extended his exploration of the Northwest Territories. His party was divided into two groups; the southern one, under Anderson, did survey and scientific work on the north mainland coast from Alaska eastward to Coronation Gulf, while the northern group traveled extensively in the northwest, discovering the last unknown islands of Canada's Arctic Archipelago: Borden, Brock, Meighen, and Lougheed. Stefansson's knowledge of the Canadian Arctic led him to predict that the area would become economically important. In World

War II he was an adviser to the U.S. government, surveyed defense conditions in Alaska, and prepared reports and manuals for the armed forces. From 1947 he was Arctic consultant at Dartmouth College, Hanover, New Hampshire. He wrote a number of books, including *My Life with the Eskimo* (1913), *The Friendly Arctic* (1921), *Unsolved Mysteries of the Arctic* (1939), and *Discovery* (1964).

LINCOLN ELLSWORTH

(b. May 12, 1880, Chicago, Illinois, U.S.—
d. May 26, 1951, New York, New York)

The American explorer, engineer, and scientist Lincoln Ellsworth (originally William Linn Ellsworth) led the first trans-Arctic (1926) and trans-Antarctic (1935) air crossings.

A wealthy adventurer, Ellsworth was a surveyor and engineer in Canada for five years (1903–08), worked for three years with the U.S. Biological Survey, and served in the U.S. Army in World War I, training as an aviator. In 1924 he led the Johns Hopkins University (Baltimore, Maryland) trans-Andean topographic survey from the Amazon River basin to the Pacific Ocean shores of Peru.

Fascinated with polar air exploration, Ellsworth financed and accompanied two such expeditions with the Norwegian explorer Roald Amundsen. On the first (1925) they reached latitude 87°44' N in two amphibian planes; an emergency landing without radio caused them to be given up for lost. With 30 days of grim effort, they carved out a takeoff field on the rough polar ice pack, after which one plane, over-loaded with the total party of six, returned to Spitsbergen (now Svalbard), off northern Norway. The following year Ellsworth and Amundsen, along with the Italian explorer Umberto Nobile, made the first crossing of the North Polar Basin in the dirigible Norge—a 3,393-mile (5,463-km) journey from Spitsbergen to Alaska that won worldwide acclaim. In 1931 Ellsworth made an 800-mile (1,300-km) canoe trip through central Labrador and later that year, for the American Geographical Society, made flights over Franz Josef Land and Novaya Zemlya—Arctic islands north of the Soviet Union.

In late 1935, on the third of four private expeditions to the Antarctic, Ellsworth and Canadian pilot Herbert Hollick-Kenyon flew across the continent from the Antarctic Peninsula to the abandoned Little America base on the Ross Ice Shelf. The two, often beset by bad weather, flew for some two weeks, and their plane ran out of fuel before they got to the base. They reached it only after a harrowing 11-day journey to the base on foot, and they were eventually retrieved in mid-January 1936 by a party sent out to find them. The area they covered during the flight, including the Sentinel Range of the Ellsworth Mountains, is now named Ellsworth Land and Marie Byrd Land. In 1939 he again flew over Antarctica and named the American Highland in the Indian Ocean quadrant.

SIR DOUGLAS MAWSON

(b. May 5, 1882, Shipley, Yorkshire, England—
d. October 14, 1958, Adelaide, South Australia,
Australia)

Sir Douglas Mawson was an Australian geologist and explorer whose travels in the Antarctic earned him worldwide acclaim.

Mawson received a bachelor's degree in mining engineering from Sydney University in 1902, and his field investigations in the Broken Hill mining area of west-central New South Wales earned him a doctorate in science from the university in 1909. A member of the scientific staff of Sir Ernest Henry Shackleton's Antarctic Expedition (1907), Mawson, together with T.W.E. David, reached the south magnetic pole on the high ice plateau of Victoria Land on January 16, 1909, making the landmark journey by sledge. From 1911 to 1914 Mawson led the Australasian Antarctic Expedition and from 1929 to 1931 directed the combined British, Australian, and New Zealand Antarctic Expedition. His explorations enabled Australia to claim some 2,500,000 square miles (6,475,000 square km) of the Antarctic continent. For his achievements as an explorer and scientist, he was knighted in 1914. In addition to his other activities, Mawson edited and contributed to the 22-volume *Reports of Australasian Antarctic Expeditions*. Another of his most notable works was the book *The Home of the Blizzard* (1915).

ROY CHAPMAN ANDREWS

(b. January 26, 1884, Beloit, Wisconsin, U.S.—
d. March 11, 1960, Carmel, California)

The naturalist, explorer, and author Roy Chapman Andrews led many important scientific expeditions for which he obtained financial support through his public lectures and books, particularly on Central and East Asia.

After graduating from Beloit (Wisconsin) College in 1906, he took a position at the American Museum of Natural History in New York City. In 1908 he went on his first expedition, to Alaska, and on that trip and until 1914 he specialized in the study of whales and other aquatic mammals; through his efforts the museum's collection of cetaceans became one of the best in the world. In 1909–10 he was a naturalist on the USS *Albatross* on its voyage to the Dutch East Indies (now Indonesia); in 1911–12 he explored northern Korea and in 1913 participated in the Borden Alaska expedition.

While serving as chief of the division of Asiatic exploration of the American Museum of Natural History, he led three expeditions, to Tibet, southwestern China, and Burma (now Myanmar; 1916–17); to northern China and Mongolia (1919); and to Central Asia (1921–22 and 1925). Numerous important discoveries were made on the third Asian expedition: the first known dinosaur eggs; a skull and other parts of *Baluchitherium* (now known as *Indricotherium*), the largest known land mammal; extensive deposits of fossil mammals and reptiles previously unknown; evidence of prehistoric human life; and geological strata previously unexplored in that region.

Andrews was the director of the American Museum of Natural History from 1935 to 1942, when he resigned in order to write. His books include *Whale Hunting with Gun and Camera* (1916), *Camps and Trails in China* (1918), *Across Mongolian Plains* (1921; with Yvette Borup Andrews), *On the Trail of Ancient Man* (1926), *Ends of the Earth* (1929), *The New Conquest of Central Asia* (1933), *This Business of Exploring* (1935), *This Amazing Planet* (1940), the autobiographical *Under a Lucky Star* (1943) and *An Explorer Comes Home* (1947), and *Beyond Adventure* (1954).

AUGUSTE PICCARD

(b. January 28, 1884, Basel, Switzerland—
d. March 24, 1962, Lausanne)

Auguste Piccard was a Swiss-born Belgian physicist who was notable for his exploration of both the upper stratosphere and the depths of the sea in ships of his own design. In 1930 he built a balloon to study cosmic rays. In 1932 he developed a new cabin design for balloon flights, and in the same year he ascended to 55,800 feet (17,000 metres). He completed a bathyscaphe in 1948 and later made several dives with his son Jacques.

Piccard was born into a family of Swiss scholars. His father, Jules Piccard, was a professor of chemistry at the University of Basel. Auguste and his twin brother, Jean, enrolled together at the Swiss Federal Institute of Technology, in Zürich, where they studied physics and chemistry, respectively. When they became doctors of science, both decided to teach in universities; Jean, the chemist, went first to Munich, then to Lausanne, and finally to the United States; and Auguste, the physicist, stayed on at the Institute. In 1920 Auguste married the daughter of a French historian at the Sorbonne (Universities of Paris I–XIII).

Piccard became interested in balloon ascents as a means of making experiments. He participated in many important research studies, and when the University of Brussels created a chair for applied physics in 1922,

Piccard, who was also a mechanic and an engineer, readily accepted the post. Having studied cosmic rays, he conceived of an experiment for observing them at ascents above 52,500 feet (16,000 metres). Previous ascents had shown that the stratosphere could be fatal and that to penetrate the isothermal layer, with its low atmospheric pressure, a revolutionary balloon would be necessary. He built such a balloon in 1930, with Belgian financing. Its main innovative feature was an airtight cabin, equipped with pressurized air; this technique later became commonplace on airplanes. Another innovation was the design of a very large balloon having sufficient ascent strength so that, on departure, it need not be completely filled.

On May 27, 1931, Piccard and Paul Kipfer reached an altitude of 51,775 feet (15,781 metres), where the atmospheric pressure is about one-tenth that at sea level. Upon returning to the surface, the scientist-adventurers were received triumphantly in Zürich and then Brussels. In 1932, in a new cabin equipped with a radio, Piccard was able to reach an altitude of 55,800 feet (17,000 metres). The following year, using the same technique but with bigger balloons, other balloonists rose to about 60,700 feet (18,500 metres) in the Soviet Union and about 61,000 feet (18,600 metres) in the United States.

As a child, Piccard had been fascinated by accounts of marine fish and thought that humans should also descend into the depths. Now, after his aeronautical successes, he wanted to build a device capable of resisting the pressures of the ocean depths, the bathyscaphe. Depth-resistant cabins are, of necessity, heavier than water. Before Piccard, they had been suspended from a cable, but at great depths this procedure was not dependable. Piccard revolutionized the dive by the principle of the balloon. Just as a lighter-than-air balloon carried the nacelle, or balloon gondola, a lighter-than-water float would support the cabin. And just as the balloon required a release of ballast to rise, the bathyscaphe would release weight in order to ascend after having completed its dive. Air, because it is too easily compressed, was not used in the floats; Piccard chose heptane (a petroleum derivative).

World War II interrupted the construction of the bathyscaphe, which was not completed until 1948. On October 26, 1948, an unpiloted trial dive with the bathyscaphe was conducted successfully in shallow waters of 80 feet (24 metres). On November 3, in a deeper dive of approximately 4,600 feet (1,400 metres), the cabin withstood the pressure perfectly, but the float was severely damaged by a heavy swell of water that it encountered after the dive. The bathyscaphe project was subsequently troubled by various difficulties until Jacques Piccard, Auguste's son, intervened.

Auguste Piccard stands within the pressurized balloon cabin he designed for flight into the upper stratosphere.
Popperfoto/Getty Images

Jacques, an assistant in the economics department at the University of Geneva, had already conducted the negotiations with the French government. Then, while in Trieste for the purpose of preparing a study of that port, he received an unexpected offer from that city's local industry to build a new bathyscaphe. Thus, in August 1953, two bathyscaphes competed in the Mediterranean: one at Toulon, France, and the other near Naples, Italy. The French-based craft descended to about 6,900 feet (2,100 metres), and the Italian-based craft reached a depth of some 10,300 feet (3,150 metres). At the age of 69, Auguste Piccard had realized his dream. His son, abandoning economics, followed in his father's footsteps and collaborated in future work with bathyscaphes. In 1954 Piccard retired from teaching and left Brussels for his native Switzerland. His grandson Bernard Piccard made the first round-the-world balloon flight in 1999.

JEAN-FELIX PICCARD

(b. January 28, 1884, Basel, Switzerland—
d. January 28, 1963, Minneapolis, Minnesota, U.S.)

Jean-Felix Piccard was a Swiss-born American chemical engineer and balloonist who conducted stratospheric flights for the purpose of cosmic-ray research.

The twin brother of Auguste Piccard, Jean-Felix graduated (1907) from the Swiss Federal Institute of Technology with a degree in chemical engineering and then earned a doctorate in natural science (1909). He taught at the universities of Munich (1914), Lausanne (1914–16, 1919–25), and Chicago (1916–18). He became a U.S. citizen in 1931 and lectured in aeronautical engineering at the University of Minnesota from 1936 until his retirement in 1952.

Jean-Felix made his first balloon ascent in 1913 with his twin brother. On October 23, 1934, with his wife, he made the first successful stratosphere flight through clouds, ascending to a height of about 11 miles (18 km). In 1937 he made an ascent of some 11,000 feet (3,350 metres) to test a metal gondola attached to a cluster of 98 balloons. Later he developed a frost-resistant window for balloon gondolas and an electronic system for emptying ballast bags.

Umberto Nobile

(b. January 21, 1885, Lauro, near Salerno, Italy—d. July 30, 1978, Rome)

Umberto Nobile was an Italian aeronautical engineer and pioneer in Arctic aviation who in 1926, with the Norwegian explorer Roald Amundsen and Lincoln Ellsworth of the United States flew over the North Pole in the dirigible Norge, from Spitsbergen (now Svalbard), north of Norway, to Alaska.

As a general in the Italian air force and a professor of aeronautical engineering at the University of Naples in 1928, Nobile began a new series of flights over unexplored Arctic regions with a craft similar to the Norge. In May 1928, on the third flight, the airship crashed on the ice north-northeast of Spitsbergen. Though Nobile and 7 companions were rescued, 17 lives were lost. (While attempting to find Nobile and his men, Amundsen disappeared, and it is believed that his aircraft crashed.) When an Italian inquiry found Nobile responsible for the disaster, he resigned his commission. In 1931 he took part in a Soviet voyage to the Arctic. After World War II the report blaming him for the 1928 crash was discredited, and he was reinstated in the air force. He resumed teaching at Naples and was a deputy in the Italian Constituent Assembly (1946). Nobile's own account of his Arctic adventures is given in *Gli italiani al Polo Nord* (1959; *My Polar Flights*).

H. SAINT JOHN PHILBY

(b. April 3, 1885, Saint Johns, Badula, Ceylon
[now Sri Lanka]—d. September 30, 1960,
Beirut, Lebanon)

The British explorer and scholar Harry Saint John Bridger Philby was the first European to cross the Rub' al-Khali, or Empty Quarter, of Arabia from east to west.

Philby was educated at Trinity College, Cambridge, and joined the Indian Civil Service in 1907. In 1917, as political officer of the Mesopotamian Expeditionary

Force, he was dispatched on a diplomatic mission to 'Abd al-'Azīz ibn Sa'ūd. After meeting with the future king of Saudi Arabia, he crossed the desert from Al-'Uqayr to Jidda—an exploit recorded in his book, *Heart of Arabia* (1922). Philby succeeded T.E. Lawrence as chief British representative (1921–24) in Transjordan (now Jordan) but resigned to establish a business in Arabia. He was an unofficial adviser of Ibn Sa'ūd and converted to Islam in 1930.

After an unsuccessful foray into politics in England in 1939 and a brief incarceration there in 1940 because of his antiwar views, Philby returned to Arabia in 1945. Ten years later he was expelled because of his public criticism of the inefficiency and extravagance of the oil-enriched Sa'ūdi regime. Philby made important contributions based on his Arabian explorations to the fields of archaeology, cartography, and linguistics. His son, Kim Philby, became a Soviet agent within the British intelligence service.

ALBERT WILLIAM STEVENS

(b. March 13, 1886, Belfast, Maryland, U.S.—
d. March 26, 1949, Redwood City, California)

The U.S. Army officer, balloonist, and early aerial photographer Albert William Stevens took the first photograph of the Earth's curvature (1930) and the first photographs of the Moon's shadow on the Earth during a solar eclipse (1932). On November 11, 1935, Stevens made a record balloon ascent with Captain (later Lieutenant

General) Orvil Anderson at Rapid City, South Dakota, attaining a height of 72,395 feet (22,066 metres). This altitude record was unequaled until 1956.

GEORGE MALLORY

(b. June 18, 1886, Mobberley, Cheshire, England—d. June 8, 1924, North Face of Mount Everest, Tibet [now in China])

The British explorer and mountaineer George Herbert Leigh Mallory was a leading member of early expeditions to Mount Everest. His disappearance on that mountain in 1924 became one of the most celebrated mysteries of the 20th century.

Mallory came from a long line of clergymen. While he was a student at Winchester College, one of the teachers recruited Mallory for an outing to the Alps, and he developed a strong aptitude for climbing. After graduating from the University of Cambridge, he became a schoolmaster, but he continued to refine his climbing skills in the Alps and in Wales. Other climbers of the era noted his natural, catlike climbing ability and his ability to find and conquer new and difficult routes.

Mallory served in France during World War I. He resumed teaching after returning to England in 1919. He had been a longtime member of Britain's prestigious Alpine Club; when the club began assembling members for the first major expedition to Mount Everest, Mallory was a natural choice.

The 1921 Everest expedition was mainly for reconnaissance, and the team had to first locate Everest before it could trek to and then around the mountain's base. Mallory and his old school friend Guy Bullock mapped out a likely route to the summit of Everest from the northern (Tibetan) side. In September the party attempted to climb the mountain, but high winds turned them back at the valley that came to be called the North Col.

Mallory also was part of the second expedition, mounted in 1922, which featured the major innovation of using supplemental (bottled) oxygen on some of the ascents. Mallory and his team climbed without supplemental oxygen and reached a height of 27,300 feet (8,230 metres) but could go no farther. A second attempt a few days later ended disastrously when his party was caught in an avalanche that killed seven porters.

In 1924 Mallory was selected for the third expedition, though he was less certain about returning. Before he left he was asked why climbers struggled to scale Everest, to which he gave the famous reply, "Because it's there." The expedition had a difficult time with high winds and deep snows. On June 6 he and a young and less-experienced climber, Andrew Irvine, set off for an attempt on the summit. The two started out from their last camp at 26,800 feet (8,170 metres) on the morning of June 8. Another member of the expedition claimed to have caught a glimpse of the men climbing in the early afternoon when the mists briefly cleared. Mallory and Irvine were never seen again. The British public was shocked at Mallory's loss.

The mystery of their fateful climb has been debated since that day, especially whether Mallory and Irvine had reached the summit. In the 1930s Irvine's ice axe was found at about 27,700 feet (8,440 metres), and in 1975 a Chinese climber discovered a body that he described as being that of an Englishman. In addition, an oxygen canister from the

1920s was found in 1991. With these clues, an expedition set out in 1999 to search for the two. Mallory's body was found at 26,760 feet (8,155 metres), and it was determined that he had died after a bad fall; Irvine was not found. It was hoped that the camera Mallory had with him would be recovered and that it might reveal if he and Irvine had made it to the top. Effects such as an altimeter, pocket-knife, and letters were found but no camera. His body was buried where it had been discovered.

T.E. LAWRENCE

(b. August 15, 1888, Tremadoc, Caernarvonshire, Wales—d. May 19, 1935, Clouds Hill, Dorset, England)

The British archaeological scholar, military strategist, and author Thomas Edward Lawrence—also called, from 1927, T.E. Shaw, but best known as Lawrence of Arabia—achieved world renown for his legendary war activities in the Middle East during World War I and for his account of those activities in *The Seven Pillars of Wisdom* (1926).

EARLY LIFE

Lawrence was the son of Sir Thomas Chapman and Sara Maden, the governess of Sir Thomas' daughters at Westmeath, with whom he had escaped from both marriage and Ireland. As "Mr. and Mrs. Lawrence," the couple had five sons (Thomas Edward was the second) during what was outwardly a marriage with all the benefits of clergy. In 1896 the family settled in Oxford, where T.E. (he preferred the initials to the names) attended the High School and Jesus College. Medieval military architecture was his first interest, and he pursued it in its historical settings, studying crusader castles in France and (in 1909) in Syria and Palestine and submitting a thesis on the subject that won him first-class honours in history in 1910. (It was posthumously published, as *Crusader Castles*, in 1936.) As a protégé of the Oxford archaeologist D.G. Hogarth, he acquired a demyship (traveling fellowship) from Magdalen College and joined an expedition excavating the Hittite settlement of Carchemish on the Euphrates, working there from 1911 to 1914, first under Hogarth and then under Sir Leonard Woolley, and using his free time to travel on his own and get to know the language and the people. Early in 1914 he and Woolley, and Capt. S.F. Newcombe, explored northern Sinai, on the Turkish frontier east of Suez. Supposedly a scientific expedition, and in fact sponsored by the Palestine Exploration Fund, it was more a map-making reconnaissance from Gaza to Aqaba, destined to be of almost immediate strategic value. The cover study was nevertheless of authentic scholarly significance; written by Lawrence and Woolley together, it was published as *The Wilderness of Zin* in 1915.

In August 1914, the month World War I began, Lawrence became a civilian employee of the Map Department of the War Office in London, charged with preparing a militarily useful map of Sinai. By December 1914 he was a lieutenant in Cairo. Experts on Arab affairs—especially those who had traveled in the Turkish-held Arab lands—were rare, and he was assigned to intelligence, where he spent more than a year, mostly interviewing prisoners, drawing maps, receiving and processing data from agents behind enemy lines, and producing a handbook on the Turkish Army. When, in mid-1915, his brothers Will and Frank were killed in action in France, T.E. was reminded cruelly of the more active front in the West. Egypt at the time was the staging area for Middle Eastern military operations of prodigious inefficiency; a trip to Arabia convinced Lawrence of an alternative method of undermining Germany's Turkish ally. In October 1916 he had accompanied the diplomat Sir Ronald Storrs on a mission to Arabia, where Ḥusayn ibn ʿAlī, amīr of Mecca, had the previous June proclaimed a revolt against the Turks. Storrs and Lawrence consulted with Ḥusayn's son Abdullah, and Lawrence received permission to go on to consult further with another son, Fayṣal, then commanding an Arab force southwest of Medina. Back in Cairo in November, Lawrence urged his superiors to abet the efforts at rebellion with arms and money and to make use of the dissident shaykhs by meshing their aspirations for independence with general military strategy. He rejoined Fayṣal's army as political and liaison officer.

GUERRILLA LEADER

Lawrence was not the only officer to become involved in the incipient Arab rising, but from his own small corner of the Arabian Peninsula he quickly became—especially from his own accounts—its brains, its organizing force, its liaison with Cairo, and its military technician. His small but irritating second front behind the Turkish lines was a hit-and-run guerrilla operation, focusing on the mining of bridges and supply trains and the appearance of Arab units first in one place and then another, tying down enemy forces that otherwise would have been deployed elsewhere, and keeping the Damascus-to-Medina railway largely inoperable, with potential Turkish reinforcements thus helpless to crush the uprising. In such fashion Lawrence—"Amīr Dynamite" to the admiring Bedouins—committed the cynical, self-serving shaykhs for the moment to his kingmaker's vision of an Arab nation, goaded them with examples of his own self-punishing personal valour when their spirits flagged, bribed them with promises of enemy booty and British gold sovereigns.

Aqaba—at the northernmost tip of the Red Sea—was the first major victory for the Arab guerrilla forces; they seized it after a two-month march on July 6, 1917. Thenceforth, Lawrence attempted to coordinate Arab movements with the campaign of General Sir Edmund Allenby, who was advancing toward Jerusalem, a tactic only partly successful. In November Lawrence was captured at Darʿā by the Turks while reconnoitring the area in Arab dress. Apparently he was recognized, and subsequently was homosexually brutalized before he was able to escape. The experience, variously reported or disguised by him afterward, left real scars as well as wounds upon his psyche from which he never recovered. The next month, nevertheless, he took part in the victory parade in Jerusalem and then returned to increasingly successful actions in which Fayṣal's forces nibbled their way north, and Lawrence rose to the rank of lieutenant colonel with the Distinguished Service Order (DSO).

By the time the motley Arab army reached Damascus in October 1918, Lawrence was physically and emotionally exhausted, having forced body and spirit to the breaking point too often. He had been wounded numerous times, captured, and tortured; had endured extremities of hunger, weather, and disease; had been driven by military necessity to commit atrocities upon the enemy; and had witnessed in the chaos of Damascus the defeat of his aspirations for

T.E. Lawrence, known as "Lawrence of Arabia," wearing a traditional Arabian headdress. Hulton Archive/Getty Images

the Arabs in the very moment of their triumph, their seemingly incurable factionalism rendering them incapable of becoming a nation. (Anglo-French duplicity, made official in the Sykes-Picot Agreement, Lawrence knew, had already betrayed them in a cynical wartime division of expected spoils.) Distinguished and disillusioned, Lawrence left for home just before the Armistice and politely refused, at a royal audience on October 30, 1918, the Order of the Bath and the DSO, leaving the shocked king George V (in his words) "holding the box in my hand." He was demobilized as a lieutenant colonel on July 31, 1919.

ADVISER ON ARAB AFFAIRS

A colonel at 30, Lawrence was a private at 34. In between he lobbied in vain for Arab independence at the Paris Peace Conference in 1919 (even appearing in Arab robes) and lobbied equally vainly against the detachment of Syria and Lebanon from the rest of the Arab countries as a French mandate. Meanwhile, he worked on his war memoir, acquiring for the purpose a research fellowship at All Souls College, Oxford, effective (for a seven-year term) in November 1919. By that time his exploits were becoming belatedly known to a wide public, for in London in August 1919 an American war correspondent, Lowell Thomas, had begun an immensely popular series of illustrated lectures, "With Allenby in Palestine and Lawrence in Arabia." The latter segment soon dominated the program, and Lawrence, curious about it, went to see it himself.

Lawrence was already on a third draft of his narrative when, in March 1921, he was wooed back to the Middle East as adviser on Arab affairs to the colonial minister, then Winston Churchill. After the Cairo political settlements, which redeemed a few of the idealistic war-time promises Lawrence had made, he rejected all offers of further positions in government; and, with the covert help of his wartime colleague, Air Marshal Sir Hugh Trenchard, enlisted under an assumed name (John Hume Ross) in the Royal Air Force in August 1922. He had just finished arranging to have eight copies of the revised and rhetorically inflated 330,000-word text of *The Seven Pillars of Wisdom* run off by the press of the *Oxford Times* and was emotionally drained by the drafting of his memoir. Now he was willing to give up his £1,200 Colonial Office salary for the daily two shillings ninepence of an aircraft-man, not only to lose himself in the ranks but to acquire material for another book. He was successful only in the latter. The London press found him at the Farnborough base, the *Daily Express* breaking the story on December 27. Embarrassed, the RAF released him early the next month.

Finding reinstatement impossible, Lawrence looked around for another service and through the intervention of a War Office friend, Sir Philip Chetwode, was able to enlist in March 1923, as a private in the Royal Tank Corps, this time as T.E. Shaw, a name he claimed to have chosen at random, although one of the crucial events of his postwar life was his meeting in 1922, and later friendship with, George Bernard Shaw. (In 1927 he assumed the new name legally.) Posted to Bovington Camp in Dorset, he acquired a cottage nearby, Clouds Hill, which remained his home thereafter. From Dorset he set about arranging for publication of yet another version of Seven Pillars; on the editorial advice of his friends, notably George Bernard Shaw, a sizable portion of the Oxford text was pruned for the famous 128-copy subscription edition of 1926, sumptuously printed and bound and illustrated by notable British artists commissioned by the author.

MAJOR LITERARY WORKS

Lawrence's *The Seven Pillars of Wisdom* (posthumous trade edition 1935, with subsequent editions since) remains one of the few 20th-century works in English to make epical figures out of contemporaries. Though overpopulated with adjectives and often straining for effects and "art," it is, nevertheless, an action-packed narrative of Lawrence's campaigns in the desert with the Arabs. The book is replete with incident and spectacle, filled with rich character portrayals and a tense introspection that bares the author's own complex mental and spiritual transformation. Though admittedly inexact and subjective, it combines the scope of heroic epic with the closeness of autobiography.

To recover the costs of printing *Seven Pillars*, Lawrence agreed to a trade edition of a 130,000-word abridgment, *Revolt in the Desert*. By the time it was released in March 1927, he was at a base in India, remote from the publicity both editions generated; yet the limelight sought him out. Unfounded rumours of his involvement as a spy in Central Asia and in a plot against the Soviet Union caused the RAF (to which he had been transferred in 1925 on the intervention of George Bernard Shaw and John Buchan with the prime minister, Stanley Baldwin) to return him to England in 1929. In the meantime he had completed a draft of a semifictionalized memoir of Royal Air Force recruit training, *The Mint* (published 1955), which in its explicitness horrified Whitehall officialdom and which in his lifetime never went beyond circulation in typescript to his friends. In it he balanced scenes of contentment with air force life with scenes of splenetic rage at the desecration of the recruit's essential inviolate humanity. He had also begun, on commission from the book designer Bruce Rogers, a translation of Homer's *Odyssey* into English prose, a task he continued at various RAF bases from Karāchi in 1928 through Plymouth in 1931. It was published in 1932 as the work of T.E. Shaw, but posthumous printings have used both his former and adopted names.

Little else by Lawrence was published in his lifetime. His first postwar writings, including a famous essay on guerrilla war and a magazine serial version of an early draft of *Seven Pillars*, have been published as *Evolution of a Revolt* (edited by S. and R. Weintraub, 1968). *Minorities* (1971) reproduced an anthology of more than 100 poems Lawrence had collected in a notebook over many years, each possessing a crucial and revealing association with something in his life.

LAST YEARS

Lawrence's last years were spent among RAF seaplanes and seagoing tenders, although officialdom refused him permission to fly. In the process, moving from bases on the English Channel to those on the North Sea and leading charismatically from the lowest ranks as Aircraftman Shaw, he worked on improved designs for high-speed seaplane-tender watercraft, testing them in rigorous trials and developing a technical manual for their use.

Discharged from the Royal Air Force in February 1935, Lawrence returned to Clouds Hill to face a retirement, at 46, filled alternately with optimism about future publishing projects and a sense of emptiness. To Lady Astor, an old friend, he described himself as puttering about as if "there is something broken in the works...my will, I think." A motorcycling accident on May 13 solved the problem of his future. He died six days later without regaining consciousness.

Lawrence had become a mythic figure in his own lifetime even before he published his own version of his legend in *The Seven Pillars of Wisdom*. His accomplishments themselves were solid enough for several lives. More than a military leader and inspirational force behind the Arab revolt against the Turks, he was a superb tactician and a highly influential theoretician of guerrilla warfare. In addition to *The Seven Pillars of Wisdom*, his sharply etched service chronicle, *The Mint*, and his mannered prose translation of the *Odyssey* added to a literary reputation further substantiated by an immense correspondence that established him as one of the major letter writers of his generation.

RICHARD E. BYRD

(b. October 25, 1888, Winchester, Virginia, U.S.—d. March 11, 1957, Boston, Massachusetts)

U.S. naval officer, pioneer aviator, and polar explorer Richard Evelyn Byrd is best known for his explorations of Antarctica using airplanes and other modern technical resources.

LIFE

After graduating from the U.S. Naval Academy in 1912, Byrd was commissioned an ensign in the U.S. Navy. He learned flying at the U.S. Naval Air Station in Pensacola, Florida, and served in the navy with distinction until the end of World War I. After the war he developed navigational methods and equipment for NC flying boats, one of which made the navy's first transatlantic airplane flight in 1919. He also assisted with dirigibles built for transatlantic crossings. His polar career began in 1924 when he had command of a small naval aviation detachment with Commander D.B. MacMillan's Arctic expedition to western Greenland, based at Etah.

The experience of flying over sea ice and glaciers in western Greenland had fired Byrd with the ambition to fly over the North Pole. On May 9, 1926, Byrd, acting as navigator, and Floyd Bennett as pilot made what they claimed to be the first airplane journey over the North Pole, flying from King's Bay, Spitsbergen, Norway, to the Pole and back. The flight lasted 15 ½ hours, with no mishaps beyond an oil leak from the starboard engine of their Fokker trimotor airplane. For this feat they were both awarded the U.S. Congressional Medal of Honor and were acclaimed as national heroes. Some doubt always lingered over whether their plane had actually reached the North Pole, and one of Byrd's early associates, Bernt Balchen, even claimed after Byrd's death that the flight to the North Pole had been a hoax. The discovery in 1996 of the diary that Byrd had kept on his famous flight shed new light on this question. Byrd's diary entries suggest that the airplane was still about 150 miles (240 km) short of the North Pole when Byrd decided to turn back because of his concern over the oil leak. (If this is true, then credit for the first flight over the North Pole actually belongs to Roald Amundsen of Norway, Lincoln Ellsworth of the United States, and Umberto Nobile of Italy, who made a well-documented flight over the Pole in a dirigible three days after Byrd's flight.)

Byrd next aided the American aviator Charles A. Lindbergh with navigational training and the use of the specially extended runway for Lindbergh's transatlantic solo flight in May 1927. Byrd then decided to make an attempt to fly the Atlantic from west to east; and in June 1927, with three companions, he made the flight in 42 hours, crash-landing in bad weather at Ver-sur-Mer on the coast of Brittany, France. For this successful flight he was made a Commandant of the French Legion of Honour.

In 1928 he announced his decision to explore the unknown regions of the Antarctic from the air. With large financial backing from such wealthy Americans as Edsel Ford and John D. Rockefeller, Jr., his fame was such that he could inspire the American public to contribute liberally to the estimated cost of the venture, which was about $400,000.

ANTARCTIC EXPEDITIONS

Byrd's first Antarctic expedition (1928–30), the largest and best-equipped that had ever set out for that continent, sailed south in October 1928. A substantial and well-supplied base, called Little America, was built on the face of the Ross Ice Shelf, a wide plain of shelf ice fronting the Ross Sea near an indentation in the ice cliff named the Bay of Whales. Flights were made from this base over the Antarctic continent. A range of high mountains, named the Rockefeller Mountains, was discovered; and a large tract of hitherto unknown territory beyond them was named Marie Byrd Land, for Byrd's wife. On November 29, 1929, Byrd, as navigator, and three companions made the first flight over the South Pole, flying from Little America to the Pole and back in 19 hours with no mishap. Byrd was afterward promoted to rear admiral for this achievement.

In 1933–35 a second Byrd expedition visited Little America with the aim of mapping and claiming land around the Pole; he extended the exploration of Marie Byrd Land and continued his scientific observations. During the winter of 1934 (from March to August) Byrd spent five months alone in a hut at a weather station named Bolling Advance Base, buried beneath the ice shelf face 123 miles (196 km) south of Little America, enduring temperatures between -58° and -76° F (-50° and -60° C) and sometimes much lower. He was finally rescued in a desperately sick condition, suffering from frostbite and carbon monoxide poisoning. This was perhaps his most controversial exploit.

At the request of President Franklin D. Roosevelt, Byrd took command of the U.S. Antarctic service and led a third expedition to Antarctica in 1939–41, this one financed and sponsored by the U.S. government. Bases were located at Little America and Stonington Island, off the Antarctic Peninsula. Byrd's discovery of Thurston Island greatly decreased the length of unexplored coast of the continent.

During World War II Byrd served on the staff of the chief of naval operations and, among other duties, evaluated Pacific islands as operational sites. After the war Byrd was placed in charge of the U.S. Navy's Operation High Jump. This Antarctic expedition, his fourth, was the largest and most ambitious exploration of that continent yet attempted and involved 4,700 personnel, 13 ships (including an aircraft carrier), and 25 airplanes. Operation High Jump's ship- and land-based aircraft mapped and photographed some 537,000 square miles (1,390,000 square km) of the Antarctic coastline and interior, much of it never seen before. Byrd flew into Little America from the deck of the aircraft carrier Philippine Sea north of the ice pack, about 700 miles (1,100 km) from the camp. He made a second flight over the South Pole and took part in several other flights.

In 1955 Byrd was made officer in charge of the U.S. Antarctic programs and became the senior authority for government Antarctic matters. In this capacity he helped supervise Operation Deep Freeze, a major scientific and exploratory expedition sent to the Antarctic under navy auspices as part of the program of the International Geophysical Year (1957–58). Byrd accompanied the expedition aboard the icebreaker *Glacier* and took his last exploratory flight over the South Pole on January 8, 1956.

BYRD'S ACCOMPLISHMENTS

Byrd was one of the world's foremost aviators and displayed extraordinary gifts in organizing successful expeditions to Antarctica. His major achievement was to apply the airplane, radio, camera, and other modern technical resources to these polar explorations. His five Antarctic expeditions made progressively greater use of ski-planes, ship-based seaplanes, and even helicopters (in 1946–47) to transport personnel and equipment and to carry out systematic reconnaissance and mapping programs using aerial photography. The expeditions yielded a wealth of new information about the continent, and operations High Jump and Deep Freeze in particular were milestones in the history of sustained, permanent scientific polar research. The aerial sextant and wind-drift instruments that Byrd invented in the years following World War I considerably advanced the science of aerial navigation and were of great use in his own explorations.

Byrd wrote several books about his adventures. His first work, *Skyward* (1928), contains descriptions of his 1928–30 expedition to Antarctica, his flight to the North

Pole, and his flight across the Atlantic. *Little America* (1930) is an official account of his aerial exploration in the Antarctic and his flight to the South Pole, and *Alone* (1938) describes his experiences at Bolling Advance Base. Byrd was extremely competent in public relations, and his expeditions were surrounded by a glare of publicity that made him a national hero and an internationally famous figure.

SIR GEORGE HUBERT WILKINS

(b. October 31, 1888, Mount Bryan East, South Australia, Australia—d. December 1, 1958, Framingham, Massachusetts, U.S.)

Sir George Hubert Wilkins was an Australian-born British explorer who advanced the use of the airplane and pioneered the use of the submarine for polar research. He, along with American aviator Carl Ben Eielson, made the first transpolar flight across the Arctic by airplane, as well as the first airplane flight over a portion of Antarctica, both occurring in 1928.

Wilkins studied engineering and photography in Australia before leaving for Britain in 1908. He learned to fly in 1910–12. In 1913–16 he accompanied the overland expedition of explorer-ethnologist Vilhjalmur Stefansson in the Canadian Arctic as official photographer. Following military service as a photographer during and after World War I, he served as second in command of the British Antarctic expedition to Graham Land on the Antarctic Peninsula (1920–21) and also was a naturalist on Sir Ernest Shackleton's last Antarctic expedition (1921–22). His polar explorations were interrupted when he led a British Museum biological expedition to tropical Australia in 1923–25.

In 1926 Wilkins and Eielson began a series of trial flights to test the feasibility of air exploration of the then unknown Arctic region north of Point Barrow, Alaska. On April 15–16, 1928, he and Eielson flew over unknown seas from Point Barrow to the Svalbard (Spitsbergen) archipelago north of Norway, completing the 2,200-mile (3,550-km) journey in about 20 ½ hours. For this feat he was knighted two months later. In the Antarctic (December 20, 1928), he and Eielson flew some 600 miles (970 km) south from Deception Island in the South Shetland Islands and across Graham Land, in the process discovering several new islands.

In 1931 he took the U.S. submarine *Nautilus* and navigated it under the Arctic Ocean to latitude 82°15' N, thus demonstrating that submarines could operate under the polar ice cap. He was the manager of Lincoln Ellsworth's U.S. Antarctic expeditions in 1933–39 and subsequently acted as consultant and geographer to the U.S. armed services. Following his wishes, after his death his ashes were scattered at the North Pole in March 1959 by the USS Skate, when it became the first submarine to surface there.

BESSIE COLEMAN

(b. January 26, 1893, Atlanta, Texas, U.S.—
d. April 30, 1926, Jacksonville, Florida)

Elizabeth ("Bessie") Coleman was an American aviator and a star of early aviation exhibitions and air shows.

One of 13 children, Coleman grew up in Waxahatchie, Texas, where her mathematical aptitude freed her from working in the cotton fields. She attended college in Langston, Oklahoma, briefly, then moved to Chicago, where she worked as a manicurist and restaurant manager and became interested in the then-new profession of aviation.

Discrimination thwarted Coleman's attempts to enter aviation schools in the United States. Undaunted, she learned French and at age 27 was accepted at the Caudron Brothers School of Aviation in Le Crotoy, France. Black philanthropists Robert Abbott, founder of the *Chicago Defender*, and Jesse Binga, a banker, assisted with her tuition. On June 15, 1921, she became the first American woman to obtain an international pilot's license from the Fédération Aéronitique Internationale. In further training in France, she specialized in stunt flying and parachuting; her exploits were captured on newsreel films. She returned to the United States, where racial and gender biases precluded her becoming a commercial pilot. Stunt flying, or barnstorming, was her only career option.

Coleman staged the first public flight by an African American woman in America on

Bessie Coleman, U.S. commemorative stamp, 1995.

Labor Day, September 3, 1922. She became a popular flier at aerial shows, though she refused to perform before segregated audiences in the South. Speaking at schools and churches, she encouraged blacks' interest in aviation; she also raised money to found a school to train black aviators. Before she could found her school, however, during a rehearsal for an aerial show, the plane carrying Coleman spun out of control, catapulting her 2,000 feet (610 metres) to her death.

FREYA STARK

(b. January 31, 1893, Paris, France—d. May 9, 1993, Asolo, Italy)

The British travel writer Dame Freya Madeline Stark is noted for two dozen highly personal books in which she describes local history and culture as well as everyday life. Many of her trips were to remote areas in Turkey and the Middle East where few Europeans, particularly women, had traveled before.

Stark had no formal education as a child, but she moved about with her artist parents and learned French, German, and Italian before she entered the University of London in 1912. After working as a nurse in Italy during World War I, she returned to London to attend the School of Oriental Studies. In her first major book, *The Valleys of the Assassins* (1934), Stark established her style, combining practical travel tips with an entertaining commentary on the people, places, customs, and history of Persia (now

Iran). Thereafter, she traveled extensively in the Middle East, Turkey, Greece, and Italy, where she made her home. During World War II she worked for the British Ministry of Information in Aden, Baghdad, and Cairo, where she founded the anti-Nazi Brotherhood of Freedom. She later visited Asia, notably Afghanistan and Nepal. Stark's other books include *The Southern Gates of Arabia* (1936), *Letters from Syria* (1942), *Alexander's Path* (1958), *The Minaret of Djam* (1970), several volumes of collected letters, and four volumes of memoirs. She was made Dame Commander of the Order of the British Empire in 1972.

OSA JOHNSON

(b. March 14, 1894, Chanute, Kansas, U.S.—
d. January 7, 1953, New York, New York)

Osa Helen Johnson (née Leighty) was an American explorer, filmmaker, and writer who, with her husband, made a highly popular series of films featuring mostly African and South Sea peoples and wildlife.

In 1910 Osa Leighty married adventurer and photographer Martin E. Johnson. For two years they played the vaudeville circuit with an exhibit of photographs Martin had taken in the South Pacific Ocean while accompanying writer Jack London on his voyage in the ketch the *Snark*. By 1912 the couple had accumulated the funds to return to the South Pacific islands and make a motion picture record of cannibal and head-hunting tribespeople. Thenceforward they alternated lengthy photographic trips into the field with lecture and exhibition tours at home. They were in the Solomon and New Hebrides (now Vanuatu) islands in 1914, northern Borneo (now Sabah, East Malaysia) in 1917–19 and again in 1935, and various parts of Africa in 1921–22, 1923–27, 1928–29, and 1933–34. In the field Martin Johnson was the principal photographer, and Osa was guard, hunter, and pilot. They made film records of wildlife for the American Museum of Natural History and gathered much valuable geographic and ethnological information.

Their motion pictures, which were highly successful in commercial distribution, included *Jungle Adventures* (1921), *Head Hunters of the South Seas* (1922), *Trailing African Wild Animals* (1923), *Simba, the King of Beasts* (1928), *Across the World* (1930), *Wonders of the Congo* (1931), *Congorilla* (1932), *Baboons* (1935), and *Borneo* (1937), along with numerous short features. They also collaborated on several books: *Cannibal-Land* (1922), *Camera Trails in Africa* (1924), *Lion* (1929), *Congorilla* (1931), and *Over African Jungles* (1935). On her own Johnson wrote *Jungle Babies* (1930) and *Jungle Pets* (1932).

After her husband's death in February 1937, Johnson continued the work they had begun together. In that year she led a large expedition from the motion picture studio Twentieth Century-Fox into the African bush to film sequences for the movie *Stanley and Livingstone*. She produced four more films on her own—*Jungles Calling* (1937), *I Married Adventure* (1940), *African Paradise* (1941), and *Tulagi and the Solomons* (1943)—and wrote *Osa Johnson's Jungle Friends* (1939), the nonfiction best-seller *I Married Adventure* (1940), *Pantaloons: The Story of a Baby Elephant* (1941), *Four Years in Paradise* (1941), *Snowball, the Baby Gorilla* (1942), *Bride in the Solomons* (1944), and *Tarnish: The True Story of a Lion Cub* (1945). She also designed a line of accurately detailed animal toys for the National Wildlife Federation.

CARL BEN EIELSON

(b. January 20?, 1897, Hatton North Dakota, U.S.—d. November 9?, 1929, off the coast of Siberia, Russia, U.S.S.R.)

The American aviator and explorer Carl Benjamin Eielson was a pioneer of air travel in Alaska and the polar regions. He and Australian-British polar explorer Sir George Hubert Wilkins made the first transpolar flight across the Arctic in an airplane, as well as the first airplane flight over a portion of Antarctica, both occurring in 1928.

Eielson, who had been fascinated with flying since his childhood in North Dakota, enlisted in the new U.S. Army in 1917 during World War I with the intention of becoming an aviator. He was still in flight school when the war ended, but he completed his training and left the military in early 1919. He spent much of the next three years as a barnstorming pilot before heading to Alaska in 1922 to become a high school teacher. Once there, Eielson quickly recognized the potential for aviation in Alaska and founded a commercial air service there that operated between Fairbanks and the interior. In 1924 he set up the first airmail route in Alaska, but that operation lasted only a short time before losing its government contract.

Eielson returned to North Dakota but was soon approached by Wilkins about using aircraft for polar exploration. The two subsequently undertook test flights in 1926 and 1927 before their pioneering journey on April 15–16, 1928, when they traveled some 2,200 miles (3,550 km) above Arctic ice from Barrow, Alaska, to Svalbard (Spitsbergen), an island in the Arctic north of Norway. On December 20, 1928, the pair made their pioneering 600-mile (970-km) flight over a portion of Antarctica. Eielson returned to Alaska to found another commercial aviation company, but he died shortly thereafter while attempting a rescue flight in Siberia. Mount Eielson, northeast of Mount McKinley in Denali National Park and Preserve, is named for him.

AMELIA EARHART

(b. July 24, 1897, Atchison, Kansas, U.S.—
disappeared July 2, 1937, near Howland Island,
central Pacific Ocean)

The American aviator Amelia Mary Earhart, one of the world's most celebrated pilots, was the first woman to fly alone over the Atlantic Ocean.

Earhart moved often with her family and completed high school in Chicago in 1916. She worked as a military nurse in Canada during World War I and as a social worker at Denison House in Boston after the war. She learned to fly (against her family's wishes) in 1920–21 and

Amelia Earhart after becoming the first woman to make a solo nonstop transcontinental flight across the United States, August 24–25, 1932. Encyclopædia Britannica, Inc.

in 1922 bought her first plane, a Kinner Canary. On June 17–18, 1928, she became the first woman to fly across the Atlantic, although she was only a passenger in a plane flown by Wilmer Stutz and Louis Gordon. The same year, her reflections on that flight were published as *20 Hrs., 40 Min.* She married the publisher George Palmer Putnam in 1931 but continued her career under her maiden name.

Determined to justify the renown that her 1928 crossing had brought her, Earhart crossed the Atlantic alone on May 20–21, 1932. Her flight in her Lockheed Vega from Newfoundland to Ireland was completed in the record time of 14 hours 56 minutes. After that flight, she wrote *The Fun of It* (1932). This soon led to a series of flights across the United States and drew her into the movement that encouraged the development of commercial aviation. She also took an active part in efforts to open aviation to women and end male domination in the new field.

In January 1935 she made a solo flight from Hawaii to California, a longer distance than that from the United States to Europe. Earhart was the first person to fly that hazardous route successfully; all previous attempts had ended in disaster. She set out in 1937 to fly around the world, with Fred Noonan as her navigator, in a twin-engine Lockheed Electra. After completing more than two-thirds of the distance, her plane vanished in the central Pacific Ocean near the International Date Line. Although her mysterious disappearance has since raised many questions and much speculation about the events surrounding it, the facts remain largely unknown.

SIR FRANCIS CHICHESTER

(b. September 17, 1901, Barnstaple, Devon, England—d. August 26, 1972, Plymouth, Devon)

Sir Francis Charles Chichester was a British adventurer who in 1966–67 sailed around the world alone in a 55-foot sailing yacht, the *Gipsy Moth IV*.

As a young man he worked in New Zealand as a miner, salesman, and land agent. Back in England in 1929, in December he began a solo flight by airplane to Australia. In 1931, having fitted a biplane with floats, he made the first east-west flight across the Tasman Sea from New Zealand to Australia. A plan to circumnavigate the globe by air ended in a crash in Wakayama prefecture, Japan, in which he was badly injured.

After serving in World War II as an air-navigation expert in England, he founded a map-publishing business in London. He took up ocean sailing in 1953 and won the first solo transatlantic race in 1960 in the *Gipsy Moth III* sailing from Plymouth to New York City in 40 days.

On his around-the-world voyage, he left Plymouth on August 27, 1966, sailing the 14,100 miles (22,692 km) to Sydney in 107 days. Embarking again on January 29, 1967, he returned to Plymouth around Cape Horn in 119 days, the 15,517 miles (24,972 km) being the longest passage made by a small sailing vessel without a port of call. He was knighted in May 1967 by Queen Elizabeth II. His last solo voyage in January–February 1971, from Portuguese Guinea to Nicaragua, covered 4,000 miles (6,437 km) in 22 days. He died shortly after illness in 1972 prevented him from making the solo transatlantic race. His books include the autobiography *The Lonely Sea and the Sky* (1964) and *The Gipsy Moth Circles the World* (1967).

CHARLES A. LINDBERGH

(b. February 4, 1902, Detroit, Michigan,
U.S.—d. August 26, 1974, Maui, Hawaii)

The American aviator Charles Augustus Lindbergh, one of the best-known figures in aeronautical history, is remembered for the first nonstop solo flight across the Atlantic Ocean, from New York to Paris, on May 20–21, 1927.

Lindbergh's early years were spent chiefly in Little Falls, Minnesota, and in Washington, D.C., where for 10 years his father represented the 6th district of Minnesota in the U.S. Congress. His formal education ended during his second year at the University of Wisconsin in Madison, when his growing interest in aviation led to enrollment in a flying school in Lincoln, Nebraska, and the purchase of a World War I Curtiss JN-4 ("Jenny") biplane, with which he made stunt-flying tours through Southern and Midwestern states. After a year at the army flying schools in Texas (1924–25), he became an airmail pilot (1926), flying the route from St. Louis, Missouri, to

Chicago. During this period he obtained financial backing from a group of St. Louis businessmen to compete for the $25,000 prize offered for the first nonstop flight between New York and Paris.

For the feat, Lindbergh in early 1927 had a single-engine monoplane built to his specifications in San Diego, California. Notably, it was outfitted with extra fuel tanks, including one in front of the cabin, which required him to use a periscope to see forward. On May 10–12 he flew what became dubbed as the *Spirit of St. Louis* from San Diego to New York in preparation for the transatlantic attempt. He took off from Roosevelt Field on Long Island (just east of New York City) on the morning of May 20 and headed east. After flying for 33.5 hours, he landed at Le Bourget field near Paris on the night of May 21, where he was mobbed by a large crowd that had come to greet him. Overnight Lindbergh—or "Lucky Lindy," as he came to be called—became a folk hero on both sides of the Atlantic and a well-known figure in most of the world. There followed a series of goodwill flights in Europe and America.

In Mexico, Lindbergh met Anne Morrow, daughter of the United States ambassador, Dwight Morrow. They were married in May 1929. She served as copilot and navigator for him on many flights, and together they flew to many countries of the world. During this period, Lindbergh acted as technical adviser to two airlines, Transcontinental Air Transport and Pan American Airways, personally pioneering many of their routes.

In March 1932 the Lindberghs' two-year-old son, Charles Augustus, Jr., was kidnapped from their home near Hopewell, New Jersey, and murdered. Partly because of Lindbergh's worldwide popularity, this became the most famous crime of the 1930s, and it was a major subject of newspaper attention until April 1936, when

Charles Lindbergh. Library of Congress, Washington, D.C.

Bruno Hauptmann was executed after being convicted of the kidnap-murder. The publicity was so distasteful to the Lindberghs that they took refuge in Europe.

After 1936, when he visited German centres of aviation, Lindbergh repeatedly warned against the growing air power of Nazi Germany. His decoration by the German government in 1938 led to considerable criticism, as did the speeches advocating American neutrality in World War II he made in 1940–41 after his return to the United States. Criticism of his public statements by President Franklin D. Roosevelt led Lindbergh to resign his Air Corps Reserve commission in April 1941.

When the United States entered the war in December 1941, however, Lindbergh, as a civilian, threw himself into the war effort, serving as a consultant to the Ford Motor Company and to the United Aircraft Corporation (later United Technologies Corporation). In the latter capacity he flew 50 combat missions during a tour of duty in the Pacific theatre; and later, after the end of the war in Europe, he accompanied a navy technical mission in Europe investigating German aviation developments.

The Lindberghs eventually had four more children; following World War II, the family lived quietly in Connecticut and then in Hawaii. Lindbergh continued as consultant to Pan American World Airways and to the U.S. Department of Defense. He was a member of the National Advisory Committee for Aeronautics and served on a number of other aeronautical boards and committees. He received many honours and awards, in addition to the Medal of Honor that had been awarded to him by a special act of Congress in 1927. For his services to the government, he was appointed brigadier general in the Air Force Reserve by President Dwight D. Eisenhower in 1954. His book *The Spirit of St. Louis*, describing the flight to Paris, was published in 1953 and gained him a Pulitzer Prize. He

was also the author of *We* (1927), *Of Flight and Life* (1948), and, with the French surgeon and biologist Alexis Carrel, *The Culture of Organs* (1938), concerning research on which he and Carrel had collaborated. His *Wartime Journals* (1970) is a record (not initially intended for publication) of his life during the years 1938–45.

LEAKEY FAMILY

The Leakeys were a family of renowned British-Kenyan archaeologists and paleoanthropologists known for their discoveries of hominin (member of the human lineage) and other fossil remains in eastern Africa. Notable members included Louis S.B. Leakey (b. August 7, 1903, Kabete, Kenya—d. October 1, 1972, London, England); his wife, Mary Douglas Leakey (b. February 6, 1913, London—d. December 9, 1996, Nairobi, Kenya); their son Richard Leakey (b. December 19, 1944, Nairobi); and his wife, Meave G. Leakey (b. July 28, 1942, London).

LOUIS S.B. LEAKEY

Louis Seymour Bazett Leakey, the patriarch of the family, proved through his fossil discoveries in eastern Africa that human beings were far older than had previously been believed and that human evolution was centred in Africa, rather than in Asia, as earlier discoveries had suggested. He was also noted for his controversial interpretations of these archaeological finds.

Born of British missionary parents, Louis spent his youth with the Kikuyu people of Kenya, about whom he later wrote. He was educated at the University of Cambridge and began his archaeological research in eastern Africa in 1924; he was later aided by Mary, his second wife, and their sons. He held various appointments at major British and American universities and was curator of the Coryndon Memorial Museum in Nairobi from 1945 to 1961.

In 1931 Louis began his research at Olduvai Gorge (now in Tanzania), which became the site of his team's most famous discoveries. The first finds were animal fossils and crude stone tools, but in 1959 Mary Leakey uncovered a fossil hominin that was given the name *Zinjanthropus* ("eastern man")—now generally regarded as a form of *Paranthropus* similar to *Australopithecus* ("southern ape")—and was believed to be about 1.7 million years old. Leakey later theorized that *Zinjanthropus* was not a direct ancestor of modern humans; he claimed this distinction for other hominin fossil remains that his team discovered at Olduvai Gorge in 1960–63 and that Leakey named *Homo habilis*. Leakey held that *H. habilis* lived contemporaneously with *Australopithecus* in eastern Africa and represented a more advanced hominin on the direct evolutionary line to *H. sapiens*. Initially many scientists disputed Leakey's interpretations and classifications of the fossils he had found, although they accepted the significance of the finds themselves. They contended that *H. habilis* was not sufficiently different from *Australopithecus* to justify a separate classification. Subsequent finds by the Leakey family and others, however, established that *H. habilis* does indeed represent an evolutionary step between the australopiths (who eventually became extinct) and *H. erectus*, who may have been a direct ancestor of modern humans.

Among the other important finds made by the Leakey team was the discovery in 1948 at Rusinga Island in Lake Victoria, Kenya, of the remains of *Proconsul africanus*, a common ancestor of both humans and apes that lived about 25 million years ago. At Fort Ternan (east of Lake Victoria) in 1962, the Leakey team discovered the remains of *Kenyapithecus*, another link between apes and early man that lived about 14 million years ago.

Leakey's discoveries formed the basis for the most important subsequent research into the earliest origins of human life. He was also instrumental in persuading Jane Goodall, Dian Fossey, and Biruté M.F. Galdikas to undertake their pioneering long-term studies of chimpanzees, gorillas, and orangutans, respectively, in those animals' natural habitats. The Louis Leakey Memorial Institute for African Prehistory in Nairobi was founded by his son

Richard Leakey as a fossil repository and postgraduate study centre and laboratory.

Leakey wrote *Adam's Ancestors* (1934; rev. ed., 1953), *Stone Age Africa* (1936), *White African* (1937), *Olduvai Gorge* (1951), *Mau Mau and the Kikuyu* (1952), *Olduvai Gorge, 1951–61* (1965), *Unveiling Man's Origins* (1969; with Vanne Morris Goodall), and *Animals of East Africa* (1969).

MARY DOUGLAS LEAKEY

The English-born Mary Douglas Leakey (née Nicol) made several fossil finds of great importance in the understanding of human evolution. Her early finds were interpreted and publicized by her husband, Louis S.B. Leakey.

As a girl, Mary exhibited a natural talent for drawing and was interested in archaeology. After undergoing sporadic schooling, she participated in excavations of a Neolithic Period site at Hembury, Devon, England, by which time she had become skilled at making reproduction-quality drawings of stone tools. She met Louis Leakey in 1933, and they were married in 1936. Shortly thereafter they left for an expedition to eastern Africa, an area that became the central location of their work.

Working alongside Louis Leakey for the next 30 years, Mary Leakey oversaw the excavation of various prehistoric sites in Kenya. Her skill at the painstaking work of excavation surpassed her husband's, whose brilliance lay in interpreting and publicizing the fossils that they uncovered. In 1948, on Rusinga Island in Lake Victoria, she discovered the *Proconsul africanus* skull, and, 11 years later, she found the *Zinjanthropus* skull at Olduvai Gorge.

After her husband's death in 1972, Leakey continued her work in Africa. In 1978 she discovered at Laetoli, a site south of Olduvai Gorge, several sets of footprints

Anthropologist Mary Leakey (standing), overseeing the work of a work crew at Oldavai Gorge (Tanzania) in 1965. Melville B. Grosvenor/National Geographic Image Collection/Getty Images

made in volcanic ash by early hominins that lived about 3.5 million years ago. The footprints indicated that their makers walked upright; this discovery pushed back the advent of human bipedalism to a date earlier than the scientific community had previously suspected. Among Mary Leakey's books were *Olduvai Gorge: My Search for Early Man* (1979) and the autobiographical *Disclosing the Past* (1984).

RICHARD LEAKEY

The Kenyan Richard Erskine Frere Leakey, son of Louis S.B. and Mary, was an anthropologist, conservationist, and political figure. In addition to making his own extensive fossil finds related to human evolution, he campaigned publicly for responsible management of the environment in eastern Africa.

Richard was originally reluctant to follow his parents' career and instead became a safari guide. In 1967 he joined an expedition to the Omo River valley in Ethiopia. It was during this trip that he first noticed the site of Koobi Fora, along the shores of Lake Turkana (Lake Rudolf) in Kenya, where he led a preliminary search that uncovered several stone tools. From this site alone in the subsequent decade, Leakey and his fellow workers uncovered some 400 hominin fossils representing perhaps 230 individuals, making Koobi Fora the site of the richest and most varied assemblage of early human remains found to date anywhere in the world.

Richard proposed controversial interpretations of his fossil finds. In two books written with science writer Roger Lewin, *Origins* (1977) and *People of the Lake* (1978), Leakey presented his view that, some 3 million years ago, three hominin forms coexisted: *Homo habilis*, *Australopithecus africanus*, and *Australopithecus boisei*. He argued that the two australopith forms eventually died out and that *H. habilis* evolved into *Homo erectus*, the direct ancestor of *Homo sapiens*, or modern human beings. He claimed to have found evidence at Koobi Fora to support this theory. Of particular importance is an almost completely reconstructed fossil skull found in more than 300 fragments in 1972 (coded as KNM-ER 1470). Leakey believed that the skull represented *H. habilis* and that this relatively large-brained, upright, bipedal form of *Homo* lived in eastern Africa as early as 2.5 million or even 3.5 million years ago. Further elaboration of Leakey's views was given in his work *The Making of Mankind* (1981).

From 1968 to 1989 Richard was director of the National Museums of Kenya. In 1989 he was made director of the

Leakey family patriarch Louis, with son Richard in the background, examining a skull unearthed during a Kenyan dig in 1970. Gordon Gahan/National Geographic Image Collection/Getty Images

Wildlife Conservation and Management Department (the precursor to the Kenya Wildlife Service [KWS]). Devoted to the preservation of Kenya's wildlife and sanctuaries, he embarked on a campaign to reduce corruption within the KWS, crack down (often using force) on ivory poachers, and restore the security of Kenya's national parks. In doing so he made numerous enemies. In 1993 he survived a plane crash in which he lost both his legs below the knee. The following year he resigned his post at the KWS, citing interference by Kenyan President Daniel arap Moi's government, and became a founding member of the opposition political party Safina (Swahili for "Noah's ark"). Pressure by foreign donors led to Leakey's brief return to the KWS (1998–99) and to a short stint as secretary to the cabinet (1999–2001).

Thereafter he dedicated himself to lecturing and writing on the conservation of wildlife and the environment. Another book with Roger Lewin was *The Sixth Extinction: Patterns of Life and the Future of Humankind* (1995), in which he argued that human beings have been responsible for a catastrophic reduction in the number of plant and animal species living on Earth. Leakey later collaborated with Virginia Morell to write his second memoir, *Wildlife Wars: My Fight to Save Africa's Natural Treasures* (2001; his first memoir, *One Life*, was written in 1983). In 2004 Leakey founded WildlifeDirect, an Internet-based nonprofit conservation organization designed to disseminate information about endangered species and to connect donors to conservation efforts. He also served in 2007 as interim chair of the Kenya branch of Transparency International, a global coalition against corruption.

MEAVE G. LEAKEY

The British-born Meave G. Leakey (née Epps) was the wife of Richard Leakey and part of the renowned family that for decades had pioneered hominin research in eastern Africa.

As a college student, Maeve planned to be a marine zoologist, and she earned a B.S. in zoology and marine zoology from the University of North Wales, Bangor. Finding that there was a lack of positions for women on ocean expeditions, she began graduate work in zoology, and from 1965 to 1968 she worked as a zoologist at Tigoni Primate Research Centre outside Nairobi. At the centre, which was administered by Louis Leakey, she conducted doctoral research on the forelimb of modern monkeys, and she obtained a doctorate (1968) in zoology from the University of North Wales. Soon thereafter she joined a team led by Richard Leakey to explore new fossil sites near Lake Turkana in Kenya. Meave and Richard were married in 1970, and they continued their research in the Lake Turkana area.

In 1989, when Richard shifted his attention to wildlife conservation, Meave became the coordinator of the National Museums of Kenya's paleontological field research in the Turkana basin. She was also the head of the National Museums' Division of Paleontology from 1982 to 2001. In 1994 Meave led a team that discovered the remains of a previously unknown species— *Australopithecus anamensis*—that was bipedal and, with an age of 4.1 million years, was one of the earliest hominins then known. One of Meave's interests was in examining evidence at research sites to determine how the environment might have influenced hominin evolution, such as the development of bipedalism. In 2001 Meave and colleagues reported on the discovery of a 3.5-million-year-old skull that they determined belonged to a previously unknown hominin genus and species—*Kenyanthropus platyops*. The find challenged the conventional view that the specimen's contemporary, *A. afarensis*, was in the direct ancestral lineage of *Homo sapiens*. In 2002

Maeve Leakey, Richard Leakey's wife, examines an artifact at the Kenyan National Museum in 1995. Alexander Joe/AFP/Getty Images

Meave, along with her daughter Louise, was named an explorer in residence by the National Geographic Society in Washington, D.C.

In 2007 Meave was a lead author of a study in *Nature* magazine that went against the prevailing view of the ancestral lineage of *Homo sapiens*, namely, that the species *H. habilis* evolved into *H. erectus* in linear succession. In 2000 the Koobi Fora Research Project, which Meave and her daughter codirected, had found fossil cranial specimens of *H. habilis* and *H. erectus* that dated from about 1.5 million years ago in an area east of Lake Turkana. The study suggested that the two species coexisted in the area for about 500,000 years. The discovery helped to show that the evolution of hominins was not as simple as a relatively sparse fossil record might have previously suggested. In addition to authoring many published scientific papers, Meave was coeditor of *The Koobi Fora Research Project, Volume I* (1977) and *Lothagam: The Dawn of Humanity in Eastern Africa* (2003).

ANNE SPENCER MORROW LINDBERGH

(b. June 22, 1906, Englewood, New Jersey,
U.S.—d. February 7, 2001, Passumpsic, Vermont)

The American writer and aviator Anne Spencer Morrow Lindbergh was perhaps best known as the wife of Charles Lindbergh—the pilot who in 1927 made the first solo transatlantic flight—and the mother of the 20-month-old baby whose kidnapping and subsequent murder in 1932 was sensationalized in the press and labeled the "crime of the century." In her own right, however, she was a renowned pilot and the author of a number of popular books of fiction, diaries, and poetry. Her best-known work, *Gift from the Sea* (1955)—a series of meditative essays on the struggle, especially by women, to achieve balance and serenity in life—sold more than five million copies in its first 20 years in print.

Lindbergh met her husband when he was her family's guest during the Christmas 1927 season. She graduated from Smith College, Northampton, Massachusetts, in 1928, and the couple were married the following year. Lindbergh took up flying herself and in 1930 became the first woman in the United States to be granted a glider pilot's license. She became her husband's copilot, navigator, and radio operator and in 1930 helped him set a new transcontinental speed record of 14 hours 45 minutes from Los Angeles to New York City. In 1931 they made a three-month-long journey to survey air routes over Canada and Alaska to East Asia, and that trip later became the subject of Anne Lindbergh's first book, *North to the Orient* (1935), which was an instant success. She solidified her reputation with her second book, *Listen! The Wind* (1938), which recounted a 1933–34 survey of transatlantic air routes.

The excessive attention surrounding their first son's kidnap-murder and the trial and death sentence of accused killer Bruno Hauptmann, as well as threats made on the life of their second son, had prompted the family to move to England in 1935, and they remained in Europe until the eve of World War II. Lindbergh's controversial next book, *The Wave of the Future, a Confession of Faith* (1940), supported the isolationist stance her husband was taking and diminished her popularity for a time, but her first novel, *The Steep Ascent* (1944), was well received, and *Gift from the Sea* spent many weeks on the best-seller list. Later works included *The Unicorn, and Other Poems, 1935–1955* (1956) and her five volumes of diaries covering the years 1922–44: *Bring Me a Unicorn* (1972), *Hour of Gold, Hour of Lead* (1973), *Locked Rooms and Open Doors* (1974), *The Flower and the Nettle* (1976), and *War Within and Without* (1980).

SIR VIVIAN ERNEST FUCHS

(b. February 11, 1908, Freshwater, Isle of Wight, England—d. November 11, 1999, Cambridge, Cambridgeshire)

Sir Vivian Ernest Fuchs was the English geologist and explorer who led the historic British Commonwealth Trans-Antarctic Expedition in 1957–58.

In 1929 and 1930–31 Fuchs participated in expeditions to East Greenland and the East African lakes, respectively, serving as a geologist. Between 1933 and 1934 he led the Lake Rudolf–Rift Valley Expedition that surveyed 40,000 square miles (104,500 square km) of the Ethiopia-Kenya region. Fuchs's thesis on the tectonics (i.e., crustal structure) of the Rift Valley earned him a Ph.D. in geology from the University of Cambridge in 1935.

Selected to head the Falkland Islands Dependencies Surveys in 1947, Fuchs became interested in Antarctica. In 1958 his 12-man party completed the first land journey across Antarctica, enduring severe hardships to travel 2,500 miles (4,000 km) from the Filchner Ice Shelf to McMurdo Sound in 99 days. The findings of the expedition confirmed earlier theories that a single continental landmass exists beneath the Antarctic polar ice sheet. With Sir Edmund Hillary, the New Zealand explorer, he coauthored the book *The Crossing of Antarctica* (1958). Fuchs later ran the British Antarctic Survey (1958–73), and in 1990 his autobiography, *A Time to Speak*, was published. He was knighted in 1958.

JACQUES-YVES COUSTEAU

(b. June 11, 1910, Saint-André-de-Cubzac, France—d. June 25, 1997, Paris)

The French naval officer and ocean explorer Jacques-Yves Cousteau was known for his extensive underseas investigations. He was also involved in the development of equipment used in underwater diving.

After graduating from France's naval academy in 1933, he was commissioned a second lieutenant. However, his plans to become a navy pilot were undermined by an almost fatal automobile accident in which both his arms were broken. Cousteau, not formally trained as a scientist, was drawn to undersea exploration by his love both of the ocean and of diving. In 1943 Cousteau and French engineer Émile Gagnan developed the first fully automatic compressed-air Aqua-Lung (scuba apparatus), which allowed divers to swim freely underwater for extended periods of time. Cousteau helped to invent many other tools useful to oceanographers, including the diving saucer (an easily maneuverable small submarine for seafloor exploration) and a number of underwater cameras.

Cousteau served in World War II as a gunnery officer in France and, later, was a member of the French Resistance against the German occupation of the country. He later was awarded the Legion of Honour for his espionage work. Cousteau's experiments with underwater filmmaking began during the war. Cousteau helped found the French navy's Undersea Research Group in 1945. He also was involved in conducting oceanographic research at a centre in Marseille, France. When the war ended, he continued working for the French navy, heading the Undersea Research Group at Toulon.

To expand his work in marine exploration, he founded numerous marketing, manufacturing, engineering, and research organizations, which were incorporated in 1973 as the Cousteau Group. In 1950 Cousteau converted a British minesweeper into the *Calypso*, an oceanographic research ship, aboard which he and his crew carried out numerous expeditions. Cousteau eventually popularized oceanographic research and the sport of scuba diving in the book *Le Monde du silence* (1952; *The Silent World*), written with Frédéric Dumas. Two years later he adapted the book into a documentary film that won both the Palme d'Or at the 1956 Cannes international film festival and an Academy Award in 1957, one of three Oscars his films received. Also in 1957, Cousteau became director of the Oceanographic Museum of Monaco. He led the Conshelf Saturation Dive Program, conducting experiments in which men live and work for extended periods of time at considerable depths along the continental shelves. The undersea laboratories were called Conshelf I, II, and III.

Adventurer and oceanographer Jacques Cousteau prepares for a dive in 1965.
AFP/Getty Images

Cousteau produced and starred in many television programs, including the American series "The Undersea World of Jacques Cousteau" (1968–76). In 1974 he formed the Cousteau Society, a nonprofit environmental group dedicated to marine conservation. In addition to *The Silent World*, Cousteau also wrote *Par 18 mètres de fond* (1946; *Through 18 Metres of Water*), *The Living Sea* (1963), *Three Adventures: Galápagos, Titicaca, the Blue Holes* (1973), *Dolphins* (1975), and *Jacques Cousteau: The Ocean World* (1985). His last book, *The Human, the Orchid, and the Octopus: Exploring and Conserving Our Natural World* (2007), was published posthumously.

TENZING NORGAY

(b. May 15, 1914, Tshechu, Tibet [now Tibet Autonomous Region, China]—d. May 9, 1986, Darjeeling [now Darjiling], West Bengal, India)

Tenzing Norgay (or Norkey or Norkay) was the Tibetan mountaineer who in 1953 became, with Edmund Hillary of New Zealand, the first person to set foot on the summit of Mount Everest, the world's highest peak (29,035 feet [8,850 metres]).

It is not known exactly when, how, or under what conditions the young Namgyal Wangdi (his original name) came to live in the Khumbu region of Nepal (near Everest), nor is it known when he took the name Tenzing Norgay (meaning "Wealthy-Fortunate Follower of Religion" in Nepalese). Among the ethnic Sherpas, immigrant Tibetans such as Tenzing are known as Khambas and have low status and little or no wealth. Tenzing worked for several years for an affluent family in Khumjung, and as a teen he ran away from difficult conditions and settled in Darjeeling, West Bengal, India. At age 19, having married a Sherpa, he was chosen as a porter for his first expedition; in 1935 he accompanied Eric Shipton's reconnaissance expedition of Everest. In the next few years he took part in more Everest expeditions than any other climber.

After World War II he became a sirdar, or organizer of porters, and in this capacity accompanied a number of expeditions. In 1952 the Swiss made two attempts on the southern route up Everest, on both of which Tenzing was sirdar. He went as sirdar of the British Everest expedition of 1953 and formed the second summit pair with Hillary. From a tent at 27,900 feet (8,500 metres) on the Southeast Ridge, they reached the summit at 11:30 AM on May 29. He spent 15 minutes there "taking photographs and eating mint cake," and, as a devout Buddhist, he left an offering of food. After his feat he was regarded as a legendary hero by many Nepalese and Indians. His many honours included Britain's George Medal and the Star of Nepal (Nepal Tara). *Man of Everest* (1955; also published as *Tiger of the Snows*), written in collaboration with James Ramsey Ullman, is an autobiography. *After Everest* (1978), as told to Malcolm Barnes, tells of his travels after the Everest ascent and his directorship of the Field Training Himalayan Mountaineering Institute in Darjeeling, which the Indian government established in 1954.

THOR HEYERDAHL

(b. October 6, 1914, Larvik, Norway—d. April 18, 2002, Colla Micheri, Italy)

The Norwegian ethnologist and adventurer Thor Heyerdahl organized and led the famous Kon-Tiki (1947) and Ra (1969–70) transoceanic scientific expeditions. Both journeys were intended to prove the possibility of ancient transoceanic contacts between distant civilizations and cultures. For the most part, Heyerdahl's theories have not been accepted by anthropologists.

Heyerdahl attended the University of Oslo, studying zoology and geography, but left before graduating to travel to Polynesia. It was while on Fatu Hiva in the Marquesas Islands that he began to wonder how Pacific inhabitants had reached the islands. On April 29, 1947, Heyerdahl and a small crew sailed from the Pacific coast of South America in the primitive raft Kon-Tiki. Their arrival in Polynesia three and a half months later demonstrated the possibility that the Polynesians may have originated in South America. The story of the voyage was related in Heyerdahl's book *Kon-Tiki* (1950) and in a documentary motion picture of the same name.

In 1969 Heyerdahl and a small crew crossed the Atlantic Ocean from Morocco to within 600 miles (965 km) of Central America in a facsimile of an ancient Egyptian reed boat, the Ra, thus confirming the possibility that the pre-Columbian cultures of the Western Hemisphere might have been influenced by Egyptian civilization. Again, the voyage was described by Heyerdahl in *The Ra Expeditions* (1971) and was the subject of a documentary film.

Late in 1977 Heyerdahl and an international crew embarked upon the Tigris expedition, a four-month, 4,000-mile (6,400-km) voyage in a craft made of reeds. The expedition began on the Tigris River in Iraq, traveling down the Persian Gulf, across the Arabian Sea to Pakistan, and ending in the Red Sea. The goal of the Tigris expedition was to establish the possibility that the ancient Sumerians might have used similar means to spread their culture through southwestern Asia and the Arabian Peninsula. The voyage was recorded in Heyerdahl's book *The Tigris Expedition* (1979) and in a documentary film. He subsequently led research expeditions to the Maldive Islands, to Easter Island, and to an archaeological site in Peru.

Heyerdahl's other books include *Aku-Aku: The Secret of Easter Island* (1958); *Fatu-Hiva: Back to Nature* (1974); and *Early Man and the Ocean: A Search for the Beginnings of Navigation and Seaborne Civilizations* (1979), in which he synthesized the findings of earlier expeditions and provided additional evidence for his theory of cultural diffusion.

SIR EDMUND HILLARY

(b. July 20, 1919, Auckland, New Zealand—
d. January 11, 2008, Auckland)

Sir Edmund Percival Hillary was the celebrated New Zealand mountain climber and Antarctic explorer who in 1953 became, with the Tibetan mountaineer Tenzing Norgay, the first to reach the summit of Mount Everest (29,035 feet [8,850 metres]), the highest mountain in the world.

Hillary's father was a beekeeper, an occupation he also pursued. He began climbing in New Zealand's Southern Alps while in high school. After military service in World War II, he resumed climbing and became determined to scale Everest. In 1951 he joined a New Zealand party to the central Himalayas and later that year participated in a British reconnaissance expedition of the southern flank of Everest. He was subsequently invited to join the team of mountaineers planning to climb the peak.

The well-organized expedition was launched in the spring of 1953, and a high camp from which to mount attempts at the summit was established by mid-May. After a pair of climbers failed to reach the top on May 27, Hillary and Tenzing set out for it early on May 29; by late morning they were standing on the summit. The two shook hands, then Tenzing embraced his partner. Hillary took photographs, and both searched for signs that George Mallory, a British climber lost on Everest in 1924, had been on the summit. Hillary left behind a crucifix, and Tenzing, a

Buddhist, made a food offering. After spending about 15 minutes on the peak, they began their descent. They were met back at camp by their colleague W.G. Lowe, to whom Hillary reputedly said, "Well, George, we knocked the bastard off." Hillary described his exploits in *High Adventure* (1955). He made other expeditions to the Everest region during the early 1960s but never again tried to climb to the top.

Between 1955 and 1958 Hillary commanded the New Zealand group participating in the British Commonwealth Trans-Antarctic Expedition led by Vivian (later Sir Vivian) Fuchs. He reached the South Pole by tractor on January 4, 1958, and recorded this feat in *The Crossing of Antarctica* (1958; with Fuchs) and *No Latitude for Error* (1961). On his expedition of Antarctica in 1967, he was among those who scaled Mount Herschel (10,941 feet [3,335 metres]) for the first time. In 1977 he led the first jet boat expedition up the Ganges River and continued by climbing to its source in the Himalayas. His autobiography, *Nothing Venture, Nothing Win*, was published in 1975.

Hillary never anticipated the acclaim that would follow the historic ascent. He was knighted in 1953, shortly after the expedition returned to London. From 1985 to 1988 he served as New Zealand's high commissioner to India, Nepal, and Bangladesh. Over the years numerous other honours were bestowed on him, including the Order of the Garter in 1995. Throughout it, however, he maintained a high level of humility, and his main interest came to be the welfare of the Himalayan peoples of Nepal, especially the Sherpas. Through the Himalayan Trust, which he founded in 1960, he built schools, hospitals, and airfields for them. This dedication to the Sherpas lasted into his later years and was recognized in 2003, when, as part of the observance of the 50th anniversary of his and Tenzing's climb, he was made an honorary citizen of Nepal.

JOHN H. GLENN, JR.

(b. July 18, 1921, Cambridge, Ohio, U.S.)

John Herschel Glenn, Jr., was the first U.S. astronaut to orbit Earth, completing three orbits in 1962. (Soviet cosmonaut Yury Gagarin, the first person in space, had made a single orbit of Earth in 1961.)

Glenn joined the U.S. Naval Reserve in 1942. He then joined the U.S. Marine Corps in 1943 and flew 59 missions in the South Pacific during World War II. In the Korean War, he flew 90 missions, and in the last nine days of the war, he shot down three MiGs. He graduated from the U.S. Naval Test Pilot School at Patuxent River, Maryland, in 1954 and flew on test projects involving the F-8 fighter. He made the first transcontinental flight with an average supersonic speed in 1957 when he flew from California to New York in 3 hours and 23 minutes. He was promoted to lieutenant colonel in 1959.

Of the "Mercury Seven," the U.S. military pilots selected in 1959 to be the first astronauts, Glenn was the oldest. He served as a backup pilot for Alan B. Shepard, Jr., and Virgil I. Grissom, who made the first two U.S. suborbital flights into space. Glenn was selected for the first orbital flight, Mercury-Atlas 6, and on February 20, 1962, his space capsule, *Friendship 7*, was launched from Cape Canaveral, Florida. Its orbit ranged from approximately 161 to 261 km (100 to 162 miles) in altitude. The flight went mostly according to plan, aside from a faulty thruster that

John H. Glenn, Jr. NASA

forced Glenn to control *Friendship 7* manually. A faulty switch onboard also relayed the inaccurate message to mission control that the heat shield had been released. He was told not to release the pack of retro-rockets on the rear of the spacecraft after they had fired. (Mission control hoped that if the heat shield had been released, the straps of the retrorocket pack would hold the shield long enough for Glenn to survive reentry.) Glenn made three orbits, landing nearly 5 hours after launch in the Atlantic Ocean near Grand Turk island in the Turks and Caicos Islands. He became a national hero.

Glenn retired from the space program in 1964 to seek the Democratic nomination for a U.S. Senate seat in Ohio. (Space-program observers generally believed that he would not have been allowed to fly again out of concern that a national hero be put at undue risk.) However, one month after he announced his candidacy, he slipped in the bathroom of his home and hit his head on the bathtub, severely injuring his inner ear. He withdrew from the campaign to recover. He left the Marine Corps and became the vice president for domestic corporate development of the soft drink maker Royal Crown Cola International Ltd. in 1965 and later became president of the company. In 1970 he ran for the Senate again but lost narrowly in the primary. He was elected U.S. senator from that state in 1974 and was reelected three times thereafter. Glenn was unsuccessful, however, in his bid to become the 1984 Democratic presidential candidate. During his time in the Senate, Glenn focused on nuclear proliferation, wasteful government spending, and aging.

On October 29, 1998, Glenn returned to space as a payload specialist on a nine-day mission (STS-95) aboard the space shuttle *Discovery*. The oldest person ever to travel in space, Glenn at age 77 participated in experiments on

Astronaut John H. Glenn, Jr., entering Friendship 7 to begin the first American manned mission to orbit Earth, February 1962.
NASA

the Spacehab module that studied similarities between the aging process and the body's response to weightlessness. His presence on STS-95 was controversial. NASA officials asserted that Glenn's presence would contribute to research on the aging process, but critics contended that his return to space was a publicity stunt with minimal benefits.

Glenn retired from the Senate in 1999. He helped found the John Glenn Institute for Public Service and Public Policy in 2000 (now part of the John Glenn School of Public Affairs) at Ohio State University, Columbus, where in 1998 he had become an adjunct professor in the political science department. In 2012 he was awarded the Presidential Medal of Freedom.

JACQUES PICCARD

(b. July 28, 1922, Brussels, Belgium—
d. November 1, 2008, La Tour-de-Peilz,
Switzerland)

The Swiss oceanic engineer, economist, and physicist Jacques-Ernest-Jean Piccard helped his father, Auguste Piccard, build the bathyscaphe for deep-sea exploration. He also invented the mesoscaphe, an undersea vessel for exploring middle depths.

He was born in Brussels while his Swiss-born father was a professor at the University of Brussels. After graduating from the École Nouvelle de Suisse Romande in Lausanne, Switzerland, in 1943, he studied at the University of Geneva, taking a year off in 1944–45 in order to serve with the French First Army. Upon receiving his licentiate in 1946, he taught at the university for two years before entering private teaching.

Meanwhile, he was helping his father to design bathyscaphes and in August 1953 accompanied him in the *Trieste* on a dive of some 10,300 feet (3,150 metres) off the island of Ponza, Italy. In 1956 Jacques Piccard went to the United States seeking funding; two years later the U.S. Navy bought the *Trieste* and retained him as a consultant. On January 23, 1960, he and Lieutenant Don Walsh of the U.S. Navy set a new submarine depth record by descending 35,814 feet (10,916 metres) into the Mariana Trench in the Pacific Ocean using the *Trieste*. He recounted this feat in

Seven Miles Down (1961), written with Robert Dietz. In the early 1960s, working with his father, he designed and built the first of four mesoscaphes. His first mesoscaphe, the *Auguste Piccard*, capable of carrying 40 passengers, transported some 33,000 tourists through the depths of Lake Geneva during the 1964 Swiss National Exhibition in Lausanne. In 1969 he drifted some 1,800 miles (3,000 km) along the east coast of North America in the mesoscaphe *Ben Franklin*, conducting research on the Gulf Stream for the U.S. Navy.

In his later career Piccard was a consultant scientist for several private American organizations for deep-sea research, including the Grumman Aircraft Engineering Corporation, New York (1966–71). In the 1970s he founded the Foundation for the Study and Protection of Seas and Lakes, based in Cully, Switzerland. In 1999 his son Bertrand Piccard, together with Englishman Brian Jones, completed the first nonstop circumnavigation of the globe in a balloon.

WALTER M. SCHIRRA, JR.

(b. March 12, 1923, Hackensack, New Jersey, U.S.—d. May 3, 2007, La Jolla, California)

The U.S. astronaut Walter Marty Schirra, Jr., manned the Mercury *Sigma 7* (1962) and was command pilot of Gemini 6 (1965), which made the first rendezvous in space. He was the only astronaut to fly in the Mercury, Gemini, and Apollo space programs.

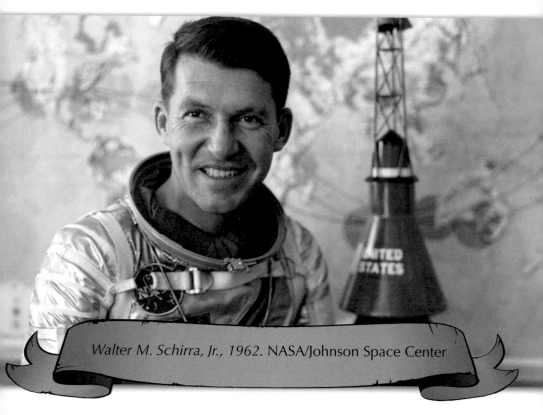

Walter M. Schirra, Jr., 1962. NASA/Johnson Space Center

Schirra began flying at 13 and became a naval aviator after graduating from the U.S. Naval Academy, Annapolis, Maryland, in 1945. He flew 90 missions in the Korean War. A test pilot, he was one of the original seven astronauts named in 1959. On October 3, 1962, Schirra orbited the Earth six times in *Sigma 7*. His scheduled flight with Thomas P. Stafford in Gemini 6 was postponed twice because of technical problems. Gemini 6 was finally launched on December 15, 1965, 11 days after Gemini 7. Schirra successfully rendezvoused with Gemini 7, maneuvering to within one foot of the craft.

Schirra commanded the Apollo 7 flight (October 11–22, 1968), accompanied by Donn Eisele and R. Walter Cunningham, on the first manned Apollo mission. They tested the guidance and control systems and the restarting capability of the rocket engines for future lunar flights.

After retiring from the navy and the space program in 1969, Schirra held executive positions in private firms in Colorado. In 2000 he was inducted into the Naval Aviation Hall of Honor.

ALAN B. SHEPARD, JR.

(b. November 18, 1923, East Derry, New Hampshire, U.S.—d. July 21, 1998, Monterey, California)

Alan Bartlett Shepard, Jr., was the first U.S. astronaut to travel in space.

Shepard graduated from the U.S. Naval Academy, Annapolis, Maryland, in 1944 and served in the Pacific theatre during World War II onboard the destroyer *Cogswell*. He earned his naval aviator wings in 1947, qualified as a test pilot in 1951, and experimented with high-altitude aircraft, inflight fueling systems, and landings on angled carrier decks. In 1957 he graduated from the Naval War College, Newport, Rhode Island. In 1959 he became one of the original seven astronauts chosen for the U.S. Mercury program by the National Aeronautics and Space Administration (NASA).

On May 5, 1961, Shepard made a 15-minute suborbital flight in the *Freedom 7* spacecraft, which reached an altitude of 115 miles (185 km). The flight came 23 days after Soviet cosmonaut Yury Gagarin became the first human to travel in space, but Shepard's flight energized U.S. space efforts and made him a national hero.

Shepard was selected as command pilot for the first manned Gemini mission, Gemini 3, but he was grounded in 1964 because of Ménière disease, an ailment that affects the inner ear. In 1969 he underwent corrective surgery that allowed him to return to full flight status.

Shepard commanded the Apollo 14 flight (January 31–February 9, 1971; with Stuart A. Roosa and Edgar D. Mitchell), which involved the first landing in the lunar Fra Mauro highlands. Near the end of his Moon walk, Shepard—an avid golfer—swung at two golf balls with a

Alan B. Shepard, Jr., in the Mercury Freedom 7 capsule May 5, 1961. NASA

makeshift six-iron club as a playful demonstration for live television cameras of the weak lunar gravity.

Shepard headed NASA's astronaut office from 1963 to 1969 and then from 1971 to 1974, when he retired from the navy as a rear admiral and from the space program to undertake a career in private business in Texas. He received numerous awards, including the NASA Distinguished Service Medal and the Congressional Medal of Honor. He also coauthored, with fellow Mercury astronaut Deke Slayton, *Moon Shot: The Inside Story of America's Race to the Moon* (1994).

Apollo 14 astronaut Alan B. Shepard, Jr., standing by the U.S. flag on the Moon, Feb. 5, 1971. Johnson Space Center/NASA

KONSTANTIN PETROVICH FEOKTISTOV

(b. February 7, 1926, Voronezh, Russia,
U.S.S.R.—d. November 21, 2009, Moscow,
Russia)

The Russian spacecraft designer and cosmonaut Konstantin Petrovich Feoktistov took part, with Vladimir M. Komarov and Boris B. Yegorov, in the world's first multimanned spaceflight, Voskhod 1 (1964).

When Voronezh was occupied in World War II, Feoktistov, who was then only 16 years old, worked as a scout for the Soviet army. He was captured by the Germans and sentenced to death by firing squad. Shot through the neck, he feigned death and escaped from a burial trench. He later attended Moscow N.E. Bauman Higher Technical School and worked for a time as a factory engineer. In 1955 he earned the equivalent of a Ph.D. and from that time worked in the Soviet space program designing spacecraft and equipment.

Feoktistov was awarded the Order of the Red Banner of Labour after the launching of the first artificial satellite, Sputnik 1 (October 4, 1957), and again after the first successful manned flight by Yury Gagarin (April 12, 1961). During the flight of Voskhod 1, October 12–13, 1964, Feoktistov carried out extensive scientific experiments and observations beyond the capability of previous cosmonauts. Voskhod 1, in addition to being the first spacecraft to carry more than one person, was the first to carry specialists (a doctor and an engineer) and the first to make a soft landing on the ground. After the Voskhod 1 flight, Feoktistov returned to engineering and played a major role in designing the Salyut and Mir space stations.

Voskhod 1 cosmonauts (left to right) commander Vladimir Komarov, doctor Boris Yegorov, and engineer Konstantin Feoktistov on their way to the launch pad, October 12, 1964. Because of the cramped dimensions of the spacecraft, they wore no space suits. NASA

VIRGIL I. GRISSOM

(b. April 3, 1926, Mitchell, Indiana, U.S.—
d. January 27, 1967, Cape Kennedy, Florida)

Virgil Ivan ("Gus") Grissom was the second U.S. astronaut to travel in space and the command pilot of the

Virgil I. Grissom, 1964. NASA

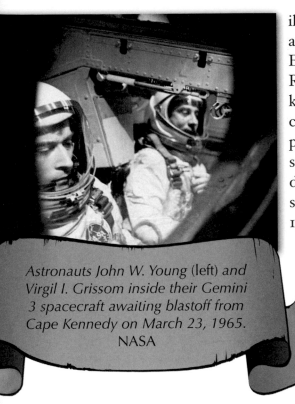

Astronauts John W. Young (left) and Virgil I. Grissom inside their Gemini 3 spacecraft awaiting blastoff from Cape Kennedy on March 23, 1965.
NASA

ill-fated Apollo 1 crew. He and his fellow astronauts Edward H. White and Roger B. Chaffee were killed, becoming the first casualties of the U.S. space program, when a flash fire swept their space capsule during a simulation of the scheduled February 21, 1967, launching of Apollo 1.

Commissioned in the U.S. Air Force in 1951, Grissom flew 100 missions in the Korean War, earning the Distinguished Flying Cross and the Air Medal with cluster. He was a test pilot and flying instructor until 1959, when he was selected as one of the original seven astronauts for Project Mercury. On July 21, 1961, with a 15-minute suborbital journey aboard the space capsule *Liberty Bell 7*, Grissom became the third man to enter space. Upon splashdown, the explosive bolts of the capsule's hatch unexpectedly opened, and Grissom immediately had to leave *Liberty Bell 7*, which sank in more than 15,000 feet (4,500 metres) of water.

On March 23, 1965, Grissom became the first man to return to space as he (as command pilot) and Lieutenant Commander John W. Young made three orbits in the first manned Gemini flight, Gemini 3. During that flight Grissom demonstrated that a space capsule could be maneuvered manually.

VLADIMIR MIKHAYLOVICH KOMAROV

(b. March 16, 1927, Moscow, Russia,
U.S.S.R.—d. April 24, 1967, Kazakhstan,
U.S.S.R. [now Kazakhstan])

The Soviet cosmonaut Vladimir Mikhaylovich Komarov is the first person known to have died during a space mission.

Komarov joined the Soviet air force at the age of 15 and was educated in air force schools, becoming a pilot in 1949. He graduated from the Zhukovsky Air Force Engineering Academy, Moscow, in 1959 and was the pilot (October 12–13, 1964) of Voskhod 1, the first craft to carry more than one human being into space.

Komarov became the first Russian to make two spaceflights when he blasted off alone on April 23, 1967, in Soyuz 1. During the 18th orbit he attempted a landing. Reportedly, the spacecraft became entangled in its main parachute at an altitude of several miles and fell back to Earth. Komarov's body was cremated, and his ashes were entombed in the wall of the Kremlin.

GENE SAVOY

(b. May 11, 1927, Bellingham, Washington,
U.S.—d. September 11, 2007, Reno, Nevada)

American explorer and amateur archaeologist Douglas Eugene Savoy discovered and explored more than 40 Inca and pre-Inca cities in Peru. Deeply interested in religious topics, Savoy also was the founder of a theology that he named Cosolargy.

At age 17 Savoy enlisted in the U.S. Navy. After World War II he attended the University of Portland and worked briefly as a journalist. He became eager to begin exploring after reading Hiram Bingham's *Lost City of the Incas* (1952). Savoy moved to Peru and organized his first archaeological expedition in 1957.

Throughout the latter half of the 20th century, Savoy made a series of expeditions to Peru, discovering various Inca and pre-Inca archaeological sites. In 1964 he discovered Vilcabamba, the secret mountain stronghold where the Incas hid from Spanish conquerors in the 16th century. His discovery disproved Bingham's notion that Vilcabamba and Machu Picchu were the same place. In 1965 Savoy took credit for the original discovery of the site he named Gran Pajatén, a pre-Inca stone city, but this finding was contested by other researchers. In 1969 he sailed a raft of ancient Peruvian design from Peru to Panama in an effort to prove that the people of the Andes had contact with the Pacific coast of Mesoamerica, and in 1997 he sailed a wooden catamaran from Peru to Hawaii to demonstrate that ancient Peruvians could have sailed on the open seas. His discovery of several thousand stone structures known as Gran Vilaya in 1985 demonstrated that the Peruvian forests—in addition to the Andes and the coast—had been locations of ancient settlement, particularly by a people known as the Chachapoya. The Gran Saposoa ruins, which Savoy brought to the world's attention after encountering them in a northern Peruvian cloud forest in 1999, added credence to this theory. Savoy wrote a number of books about his archaeological expeditions, including *Antisuyo: The Search for the Lost Cities of the Amazon* (1970).

Savoy was also intrigued by the beliefs of ancient religious groups, especially those of the Essenes, an ascetic Jewish sect that apparently revered the Sun and (he believed) presaged the coming of Jesus Christ. Developing a theology that he called "Cosolargy," Savoy proposed that Christ's Second Coming is manifest as the "spiritual Sun," a celestial force perpetually generating divine energy from the thought and will of God in order to regenerate the physical world. Illuminated by the "transformed sunlight" that carries this Christ force, human beings can become spiritual coparticipants with God in the renewal not only of themselves but of the world. In 1959 Savoy established the International Community of Christ, Church of the Second Advent to promote Cosolargy. Throughout his life he wrote more than 60 volumes on religious topics.

FRANK BORMAN

(b. March 14, 1928, Gary, Indiana, U.S.)

Frank Borman was the U.S. astronaut who, in Apollo 8 with James A. Lovell and William A. Anders in December 1968, made the first manned flight around the Moon. The astronauts remained in an orbit some 70 miles (112 km) above the surface of the Moon for about 20 hours, transmitting television pictures back to Earth and verifying that lunar landmarks could be used for navigation to lunar landing sites. Three years earlier Borman and Lovell had made the Gemini 7 endurance flight in which they remained in space for 330 hours 35 minutes. Borman and Lovell also performed the first space rendezvous, coming within a few feet of Gemini 6.

Borman graduated from the U.S. Military Academy, West Point, New York, in 1950, was commissioned in the U.S. Air Force, and served with the 44th Fighter Bomber Squadron in the Philippines between 1951 and 1956. He subsequently taught at the Air Force Fighter Weapons School. After taking his master's degree in aeronautical engineering (1957) at the California Institute of Technology, Pasadena, Borman taught at West Point and at the Air Force Aerospace Research Pilots School. In 1962 he was chosen by NASA to be a member of the second group of astronauts. After the Apollo 8 flight he became deputy director of flight crew operations for NASA.

In July 1970 Borman resigned from NASA and became a company executive of Eastern Air Lines. He was chief executive officer of Eastern from 1975 to 1986, and after Eastern's sale to Texas Air Corporation he served as vice chairman of that company until 1991. He also was on the board of the laser company Patlex from 1988 to 1996.

JAMES A. LOVELL, JR.

(b. March 25, 1928, Cleveland, Ohio, U.S.)

The U.S. astronaut James A. Lovell, Jr., was the commander of the nearly disastrous Apollo 13 flight to the Moon in 1970.

Lovell, a graduate (1952) of the U.S. Naval Academy, Annapolis, Maryland, became a test pilot. He was serving as a flight instructor and safety officer at the time (1963) he was selected by NASA for the manned space program. Lovell accompanied Frank Borman on the record-breaking 14-day flight of Gemini 7. Launched December 4, 1965, Gemini 7 was joined in space by Gemini 6, launched 11 days later and manned by Walter M. Schirra, Jr., and Thomas P. Stafford, for the first successful space rendezvous. Lovell joined Edwin E. Aldrin for the last flight of the Gemini series, Gemini 12, which was launched on November 11, 1966, and remained in orbit for four days.

Apollo 8 was launched on December 21, 1968, and carried Lovell, Borman, and William Anders on the first manned flight around the Moon. This flight was the first of three preparatory to the Moon landing of Apollo 11.

With astronauts Fred W. Haise, John L. Swigert, Jr., and Lovell aboard, Apollo 13 lifted off on April 11, 1970, headed for the Fra Mauro Hills on the Moon. On April 13, approximately 205,000 miles (330,000 km) from Earth, an explosion ruptured an oxygen tank in the service module. The resulting shortage of power and oxygen forced the abandonment of the Moon mission. Apollo 13's crew changed course to swing once around the Moon and then return to Earth. With the successful return of Apollo 13 on April 17, Lovell had completed more than 715 hours of space travel.

Lovell remained in NASA, and in 1971 he became a deputy director of the Johnson Space Center, Houston, Texas. He retired from the navy and the space program in 1973 but remained in Houston as a corporation executive until his retirement in 1991.

ANDRIYAN GRIGORYEVICH NIKOLAYEV

ANDRIYAN GRIGORYEVICH NIKOLAYEV

(b. September 5, 1929, Shorshely, Chuvash
A.S.S.R., U.S.S.R. [now Chuvashia, Russia]—
d. July 3, 2004, Cheboksary, Chuvashia, Russia)

The Soviet cosmonaut Andriyan Grigoryevich Nikolayev piloted the Vostok 3 spacecraft, launched August 11, 1962. When Vostok 4, piloted by Pavel R. Popovich, was launched a day later, there were, for the first time, two manned craft in space simultaneously. The two made radio and visual contact, but there was no attempt at docking. Both landed on August 15.

The son of a worker on a collective farm, Nikolayev studied and worked in forestry until drafted into the Soviet army in 1950. An early interest in flying persisted, and he soon transferred to the air force; in 1954 he became a pilot. In 1957 he joined the Communist Party, and in March 1960 he entered cosmonaut training. In 1962 he became the third Russian cosmonaut to travel into space, and during his 96-hour flight, which set an endurance record, he orbited Earth 64 times. Nikolayev later served as the commander of the Soviet Astronauts' Detachment.

On November 3, 1963, Nikolayev married Valentina Tereshkova, who in June 1963 had become the first woman to travel in space. They had one child and were subsequently divorced.

Nikolayev and Vitaly I. Sevastyanov manned the Soyuz 9 flight on June 1, 1970, and set a new space endurance record of almost 18 days in orbit. The mission, primarily one of determining the effects of prolonged spaceflight, ended on June 19. Nikolayev was twice named Hero of the Soviet Union.

BUZZ ALDRIN

(b. January 20, 1930, Montclair, New Jersey, U.S.)

The American astronaut Edwin Eugene ("Buzz") Aldrin, Jr., was the second person to set foot on the Moon.

A graduate of the U.S. Military Academy, West Point, New York (1951), Aldrin became an air force pilot. He flew 66 combat missions in Korea and later served in West Germany. In 1963 he wrote a dissertation on orbital mechanics to earn a Ph.D. from the Massachusetts Institute of Technology, Cambridge. Later that year he was chosen as an astronaut.

On November 11, 1966, he joined James A. Lovell, Jr., on the four-day Gemini 12 flight. Aldrin's record 5 ½-hour walk in space proved that humans can function effectively in the vacuum of space.

Apollo 11, manned by Aldrin, Neil A. Armstrong, and Michael Collins, was launched to the Moon on July 16, 1969. Four days later Armstrong and Aldrin landed near the edge of Mare Tranquillitatis and descended, respectively, to the lunar surface. After spending about two hours in gathering rock samples, taking photographs, and setting up scientific equipment for tests, they concluded their lunar surface excursion. Armstrong and Aldrin later

piloted the lunar module *Eagle* to a successful rendezvous with Collins and the command module in lunar orbit. The mission ended on July 24 with splashdown in the Pacific Ocean.

Aldrin retired from NASA in 1971 to become commandant of the Aerospace Research Pilot School at Edwards Air Force Base in California. In March 1972 he retired from the air force to enter private business. In 1988 he legally changed his name to Buzz Aldrin. ("Buzz" was his lifelong nickname.) In 1998 he founded the ShareSpace Foundation, a nonprofit organization to promote the expansion of manned space travel. He wrote two autobiographies, *Return to Earth* (1973) and *Magnificent Desolation: The Long Journey Home from the Moon* (2009, with Ken

Apollo 11 astronaut Buzz Aldrin, photographed July 20, 1969, during the first manned mission to the Moon's surface. Reflected in Aldrin's faceplate is the lunar module and astronaut Neil Armstrong, who took the picture. NASA

Abraham). He also wrote a history of the Apollo program, *Men from Earth* (1989, with Malcolm McConnell), and two children's books, *Reaching for the Moon* (2005) and *Look to the Stars* (2009).

CHARLES CONRAD, JR.

(b. June 2, 1930, Philadelphia, Pennsylvania, U.S.—d. July 8, 1999, near Ojai, California)

The American astronaut Charles P. ("Pete") Conrad, Jr., was the copilot on the Gemini 5 spaceflight (1965), command pilot of Gemini 11, spacecraft commander of the Apollo 12 flight to the Moon, and commander of the Skylab 2 mission.

Conrad enlisted in the U.S. Navy in 1953 and became a test pilot and flight instructor. In 1962 he was chosen as a member of the second group of astronauts. With command pilot L. Gordon Cooper, Jr., he took part in several new experiments during the Gemini 5 flight, which established a new manned-spaceflight record of 190 hours 56 minutes.

Manned by Conrad and Richard F. Gordon, Jr., Gemini 11 was launched on September 12, 1966, and docked with an Agena target vehicle on the first orbit. The craft then attained a record manned orbit of 850 miles (1,370 km) altitude.

On November 14, 1969, Conrad joined Gordon and Alan L. Bean on the Apollo 12 flight to the Moon. The success of the flight was characterized by the pinpoint

The crew of the Apollo 12 lunar landing mission: (left to right) Charles ("Pete") Conrad, Jr.; Richard F. Gordon, Jr.; and Alan L. Bean. NASA Great Images in Nasa Collection

landing (November 19) of the Lunar Module only 600 feet (183 metres) from the unmanned Surveyor 3 craft, which had landed there in April 1967. The total time spent on the lunar surface was 31 hours 31 minutes; Apollo 12 completed its return trip to Earth on November 24.

On the Skylab 2 mission (May 25–June 22, 1973) Conrad, Joseph P. Kerwin, and Paul J. Weitz docked their Apollo spacecraft with the orbiting Skylab, which had sustained damage during its launch on May 14. They made repairs to keep Skylab from overheating and to ensure a power supply sufficient to allow them to complete most of their assigned experimental work.

Conrad resigned from the Navy and the space program in 1974, taking executive positions, first with the American Television and Communications Corporation of Denver, Colorado, and in 1978 with the McDonnell-Douglas Corporation in Long Beach, California.

BEN L. ABRUZZO

(b. June 9, 1930, Rockford, Illinois, U.S.—
d. February 11, 1985, Albuquerque, New Mexico)

Ben L. Abruzzo was an American balloonist who, with three crewmates, made the first transpacific balloon flight and the longest nonstop balloon flight, in the *Double Eagle V*.

Abruzzo graduated from the University of Illinois (Champaign-Urbana) in 1952 and served two years in the

U.S. Air Force at Kirtland Air Force Base in Albuquerque, New Mexico (1952–54). He settled in Albuquerque and became a real-estate developer, eventually becoming the owner of two well-known ski resorts, one near Albuquerque and the other near Santa Fe. He, as well as his wife and children, became active in skiing, boating, sailing, tennis, flying, and ballooning. In 1978 Abruzzo, with Maxie Anderson and Larry Newman, made the first transatlantic balloon flight in the *Double Eagle II*. In 1979 Abruzzo and Anderson won the Gordon Bennett race in the *Double Eagle III*.

The transpacific flight, with Abruzzo as captain and teammates Larry Newman and Ron Clark, both of Albuquerque, and Rocky Aoki, a Japanese American restaurateur from Miami, who partly financed the flight, was launched from Nagashima, Japan, on November 9, 1981. The balloon landed, 84 hours 31 minutes later, in Mendocino National Forest in California on November 12. The flight covered 5,768 miles (9,244 km), the longest balloon flight in history to that date.

Abruzzo was the holder of nine world ballooning records, more than any other balloonist, at the time he and his wife, along with four companions, died in the crash of a small plane that he was piloting. His children carried on the family businesses, and his son Richard became a prominent balloonist in his own right. Richard Abruzzo and ballooning partner Carol Rymer Davis, a prominent Denver radiologist, won the 2004 Gordon Bennett race, but both were killed in September 2010, during that year's Bennett race, when their balloon crashed into the Adriatic Sea.

DONN EISELE

(b. June 23, 1930, Columbus, Ohio, U.S.—d.
December 2, 1987, Tokyo, Japan)

The U.S. astronaut Donn Fulton Eisele served as command module pilot on the Apollo 7 space mission (October 11–22, 1968), the first manned flight of the Apollo program.

Eisele graduated from the U.S. Naval Academy, Annapolis, Maryland, in 1952 and transferred to the U.S. Air Force the next year. He received an M.S. in astronautics from the Air Force Institute of Technology at Wright-Patterson Air Force Base, Dayton, Ohio, in 1960, and he joined the space program in 1964. After completing the Apollo 7 mission, Eisele was named to the backup crew of Apollo 10. He left the astronaut corps in 1970 to take up an assignment at Langley Research Center in Hampton, Virginia.

Donn F. Eisele. NASA/ Johnson Space Center

Resigning from the Air Force and the space program in 1972, Eisele became director of the Peace Corps in Thailand and later accepted executive positions in private business enterprises.

NEIL ARMSTRONG

(b. August 5, 1930, Wapakoneta, Ohio, U.S.—
d. August 25, 2012, Cincinnati, Ohio)

The U.S. astronaut Neil Alden Armstrong was the first person to set foot on the Moon.

Armstrong became a licensed pilot on his 16th birthday and a naval air cadet in 1947. His studies in aeronautical engineering at Purdue University in West Lafayette, Indiana, were interrupted in 1950 by his service in the Korean War, during which he was shot down once and was awarded three Air Medals. In 1955 he became a civilian research pilot for the National Advisory Committee for Aeronautics (NACA), later NASA. He flew more than 1,100 hours, testing various supersonic jet fighters as well as the X-15 rocket plane.

In 1962 Armstrong joined the space program with its second group of astronauts. On March 16, 1966, Armstrong, as command pilot of Gemini 8, and David R. Scott rendezvoused with an unmanned Agena rocket and completed the first manual space docking maneuver. After the docking, a rocket thruster malfunction sent the

U.S. astronaut Neil Armstrong, Apollo 11 commander, participating in simulation training in preparation for the lunar landing mission. NASA

spacecraft into an uncontrolled spin and forced them to separate from the Agena. Armstrong then regained control of the Gemini craft and made an emergency splashdown in the Pacific Ocean.

On July 16, 1969, Armstrong, along with Edwin E. Aldrin, Jr., and Michael Collins, blasted off in the Apollo 11 vehicle toward the Moon. Four days later, at 4:17 PM U.S. Eastern Daylight Time (EDT), the Eagle lunar landing module, guided manually by Armstrong, touched down on a plain near the southwestern edge of the Sea of Tranquillity (Mare Tranquillitatis). At 10:56 PM EDT on July 20, 1969, Armstrong stepped from the *Eagle* onto the Moon's dusty surface with the words, "That's one small step for [a] man, one giant leap for mankind." (In the excitement of the moment, Armstrong skipped the "a" in the statement that he had prepared.) Armstrong and Aldrin left the module for more than two hours and deployed scientific instruments, collected surface samples, and took numerous photographs.

On July 21, after 21 hours and 36 minutes on the Moon, they lifted off to rendezvous with Collins and begin the voyage back to Earth. After splashdown in the Pacific at 12:51 PM EDT on July 24, the three astronauts spent 18 days in quarantine to guard against possible contamination by lunar microbes. During the days that followed, and during a tour of 21 countries, they were hailed for their part in the opening of a new era in human exploration of the universe.

Armstrong resigned from NASA in 1971. After Apollo 11, he shied away from becoming a public figure and confined himself to academic and professional endeavours. From 1971 to 1979 he was professor of aerospace engineering at the University of Cincinnati (Ohio). After 1979 Armstrong served as chairman or director for a number of companies, among them Computing Technologies for Aviation from 1982 to 1992 and AIL Systems (later EDO Corporation), a maker of electronic equipment for the military, from 1977 until his retirement in 2002. He also served on the National Commission on Space (NCOS), a panel charged with setting goals for the space program, and on the Presidential Commission on the Space Shuttle *Challenger* Accident, the group appointed in 1986 to analyze the safety failures in the *Challenger* disaster. He was awarded the Presidential Medal of Freedom in 1969.

THOMAS P. STAFFORD

(b. September 17, 1930, Weatherford, Oklahoma, U.S.)

Thomas Patten Stafford was the American astronaut who flew two Gemini rendezvous missions (1965–66) and commanded the Apollo 10 mission (1969)—the final test of Apollo systems before the first manned landing on the Moon—as well as the Apollo spacecraft that docked with a Soviet Soyuz craft in space in 1975.

A graduate (1952) of the U.S. Naval Academy, Annapolis, Maryland, Stafford transferred to the Air Force and studied at the Air Force Experimental Flight Test School. Stafford was Walter M. Schirra's copilot on the Gemini 6 mission, launched December 15, 1965. Their rendezvous with the previously launched Gemini 7 was the world's first successful space rendezvous. On June 3, 1966, Eugene A. Cernan and command pilot Stafford were launched into space in Gemini 9. Stafford performed three rendezvous with a target vehicle, but a protective covering on the target had failed to detach, preventing docking.

Apollo 10, manned by Stafford, Cernan, and John W. Young, was launched on May 18, 1969. Three days later the spacecraft attained lunar orbit. The flight rehearsed every phase of a Moon landing except the landing itself. Cernan and Stafford descended in the Lunar Module to within 9.5 miles (15 km) of the Moon's surface. Apollo 10 completed 31 orbits of the Moon before returning to Earth, landing in the Pacific Ocean on May 26.

Stafford resigned from the space program in 1975 to become commander of the Air Force Flight Test Center, Edwards Air Force Base, California. In 1978 he was promoted to lieutenant general and became Air Force Deputy Chief of Staff for Research and Development, stationed in Washington, D.C. After retiring from the Air Force in 1979, he became an executive of a transportation company in Oklahoma.

JOHN W. YOUNG

(b. September 24, 1930, San Francisco,
California, U.S.)

The U.S. astronaut John Watts Young participated in the Gemini, Apollo, and space shuttle programs. He was the first astronaut to make five—and later the first to make six—spaceflights. He served as Virgil I. Grissom's copilot on Gemini 3 (1965), the first U.S. two-man spaceflight.

After graduating from Georgia Institute of Technology (1952) with a degree in aeronautical engineering, Young joined the U.S. Navy. He served in Korea before participating in a test project during which, in 1962, he set two time-to-climb records in an F-4B navy jet. During 1962–64 Young trained for his part in the NASA project.

Gemini 3, launched on March 23, 1965, reached a maximum altitude of 139 miles (224 km) on the initial orbit. The orbit was changed three times, and after 4 hours 53 minutes flight time the spacecraft landed in the South Atlantic Ocean. After this flight U.S. President Lyndon B. Johnson conferred the NASA Exceptional Service Medal on Young. On July 18, 1966, Young joined Michael Collins on the Gemini 10 flight. The two docked with an Agena target vehicle and, using the Agena's engine, attained an altitude of 475 miles (764 km). On May 18, 1969, Apollo 10 was launched, with Thomas P. Stafford, Eugene A. Cernan, and Young on board. The flight, which orbited the Moon, was the last checkout of Apollo systems before the Moon landing of Apollo 11. Young was commander of the Apollo 16 mission (April 16–27, 1972; with Charles M. Duke, Jr., and Thomas K. Mattingly), the fifth manned landing on the Moon. He retired from the navy in 1976 but remained with the space program, becoming chief of the astronaut office.

He was commander of the first space shuttle mission (April 12–14, 1981; with Robert L. Crippen), guiding the orbiter Columbia to a landing at Edwards Air Force Base in California after it had circled Earth 36 times. In 1983 Young commanded the joint NASA and European Space Agency mission, which from November 28 to December 8 carried Spacelab, a scientific workshop, in the *Columbia*'s payload bay. Beginning in 1987, he held management positions concerned with space shuttle operations and safety at the Johnson Space Center in Houston, Texas. He retired from NASA in 2004.

PAVEL ROMANOVICH POPOVICH

(b. October 5, 1930, Uzin, Ukraine, U.S.S.R.—
d. September 30, 2009, Gurzuf, Ukraine)

Pavel Romanovich Popovich was the Soviet cosmonaut who piloted the Vostok 4 spacecraft, launched August 12, 1962. He and Andriyan G. Nikolayev, who was launched a day earlier in Vostok 3, became the first two humans to be in space simultaneously. The two spacecraft came within 3 miles (5 km) of each other. Vostok 4 landed on August 15, 1962.

Popovich, a herdsman in his early youth, graduated from a technical school in Magnitogorsk, Russia, U.S.S.R., in 1951, when he entered the army. He quickly transferred to the air force and in 1954 graduated from the Stalingrad Air Force College. He became a pilot, and in 1960 he was among the first to enter cosmonaut training.

Popovich was also the commander of the Soyuz 14 mission (July 3–19, 1974), on which he was accompanied by flight engineer Yury P. Artyukhin. The cosmonauts docked their craft with Salyut 3, a military space station that had been placed in orbit on June 25, and engaged in a 15-day program of reconnaissance of Earth's surface. From 1980 to 1989 he was the deputy chief of the Yury Gagarin Cosmonaut Training Centre in Star City, near Moscow. He retired as a cosmonaut in 1982. At the time of his death, he was chairman of the board of the All-Russia Institute of Agricultural Aero-Photo-Geodesic Studies.

EDWARD HIGGINS WHITE II

(b. November 14, 1930, San Antonio, Texas, U.S.—d. January 27, 1967, Cape Kennedy, Florida)

Edward Higgins White II was the first U.S. astronaut to walk in space. White graduated from the U.S. Military Academy, West Point, New York, in 1952 and was commissioned a second lieutenant in the U.S. Air Force.

He took flight training and served in a fighter squadron in Germany. In 1959 he received his M.S. in aeronautical engineering from the University of Michigan, Ann Arbor, and graduated from the Air Force Test Pilot School, Edwards Air Force Base, California.

White was selected in 1962 as a member of the second group of astronauts. Often called the most physically fit astronaut, he was chosen to join James A. McDivitt on

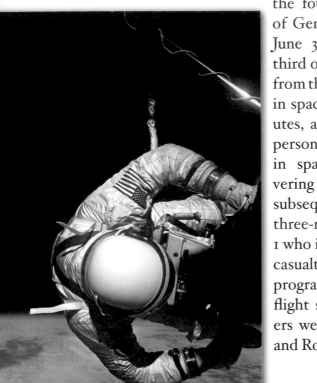

the four-day orbital flight of Gemini 4, launched on June 3, 1965. During the third orbit White emerged from the spacecraft, floated in space for about 20 minutes, and became the first person to propel himself in space with a maneuvering unit. White was subsequently one of the three-man crew of Apollo 1 who in 1967 were the first casualties of the U.S. space program, killed during a flight simulation (the others were Virgil I. Grissom and Roger B. Chaffee).

Gemini 4 astronaut Edward White during his historic 21-minute space walk on June 5, 1965. White was secured to the Gemini spacecraft by a 25-foot (7.6-metre) umbilical and tether line. He used a self-maneuvering unit to facilitate movement outside the craft. NASA

JOHN L. SWIGERT, JR.

(b. August 30, 1931, Denver, Colorado, U.S.—
d. December 27, 1982, Washington, D.C.)

The U.S. astronaut John Leonard ("Jack") Swigert, Jr., was a participant in the Apollo 13 mission (April 11–17, 1970), in which an intended Moon landing was aborted because of a ruptured fuel-cell oxygen tank in the service module. The crew, consisting of Swigert, Fred W. Haise, Jr., and Commander James A. Lovell, Jr., returned safely to Earth, making use of the life-support system in the lunar module. Swigert was a last-minute substitute for Thomas K. Mattingly, who had been exposed to measles (though he never became ill).

Swigert graduated from the University of Colorado, Boulder, in 1953 and was awarded a master's degree by the Rensselaer Polytechnic Institute, Troy, New York, in 1965. Before becoming an astronaut in 1966, he was a U.S. Air Force pilot in Japan and Korea and a commercial test pilot.

Swigert took a leave of absence from the space program in 1973 to become executive director of the Committee on Science and Technology of the U.S. House of Representatives. He resigned from the committee and from NASA in 1977 and entered private business in Virginia. He ran unsuccessfully for a seat in the U.S. Senate in 1978 but was elected from Colorado to the House of Representatives in 1982, shortly before his death.

John L. Swigert, Jr., 1966. NASA

DIAN FOSSEY

(b. January 16, 1932, San Francisco, California,
U.S.—d. December 26, 1985, Rwanda)

The American zoologist Dian Fossey became the world's leading authority on the mountain gorilla.

Fossey trained to become an occupational therapist at San Jose State College and graduated in 1954. She worked in that field for several years at a children's hospital in Louisville, Kentucky. In 1963 she took a trip to eastern Africa, where she met the anthropologist Louis Leakey and had her first glimpse of mountain gorillas. She returned to the United States after her trip, but in 1966 Leakey persuaded her to go back to Africa to study the mountain gorilla in its natural habitat on a long-term basis. To this end, she established the Karisoke Research Centre in 1967 and began a hermitlike existence in Rwanda's Virunga Mountains, which was one of the last bastions of the endangered mountain gorilla. Through patient effort, Fossey was able to observe the animals and accustom them to her presence, and the data that she gathered greatly enlarged contemporary knowledge of the gorilla's habits, communication, and social structure.

Fossey left Africa in 1970 to complete work for a doctorate at the University of Cambridge in England. In 1974 she received her degree in zoology with the completion of her dissertation, "The Behavior of the Mountain Gorilla."

She returned to Rwanda with student volunteers who made broader kinds of research possible. Motivated by the killing of Digit, one of her favoured gorillas, Fossey generated international media coverage in 1978 in her battle against poachers.

In 1980 Fossey returned to the United States to accept a visiting associate professorship at Cornell University, Ithaca, New York. While teaching, Fossey also completed *Gorillas in the Mist* (1983; film 1988). Back in Rwanda, Fossey resumed her campaign against poachers, taking increasingly drastic measures to protect the Virunga gorillas. On December 26, 1985, her slain body was discovered near her campsite. Though no assailant was ever identified, it is widely suspected that she was killed by the poachers against whom she had struggled for so long.

JOSEPH KERWIN

(b. February 19, 1932, Oak Park, Illinois, U.S.)

The U.S. astronaut and physician Joseph Peter Kerwin served as science pilot on Skylab 2, the first manned mission to the first U.S. space station.

Kerwin received his degree in medicine in 1957 from Northwestern University Medical School in Chicago, Illinois, after which he joined the U.S. Navy Medical Corps. In 1965 NASA chose him to be an astronaut.

On May 14, 1973, the unmanned Skylab space station was launched but sustained serious damage in the

Astronaut Joseph Kerwin, Skylab 2 science pilot, forming a perfect sphere by blowing water droplets from a straw in zero gravity in the crew quarters of the Skylab space station, 1973. NASA/Johnson Space Center

process. One of Skylab's solar arrays was torn off; the other did not open. A sun shield designed to keep the station cool was also torn away, causing temperatures inside to reach 129 °F (54 °C). In an effort to save the space station, Kerwin, along with commander Charles Conrad, Jr., and command module pilot Paul Weitz, were launched on May 25, 1973, from Cape Kennedy to rendezvous with Skylab. Kerwin helped repair the damaged space station and, as the first physician to participate in a U.S. spaceflight, monitored the physical effects (particularly of prolonged weightlessness) of the space environment on the crew. The astronauts successfully completed their mission and returned to Earth on June 22.

Kerwin subsequently worked at the astronaut office at the Johnson Space Center (JSC) in Houston, Texas. From 1982 to 1983 he was NASA's senior science representative in Australia, and from 1983 to 1987 he was director of space and life sciences at the JSC. He was in charge of the team that investigated the cause of death of the seven astronauts killed in the *Challenger* disaster. He left NASA in 1987 for the aerospace company Lockheed, where he managed several projects connected with the International Space Station. In 1997 he became president of Krug Life Sciences, an American company that provided medical services for the JSC. In 1998 Krug was bought by Wyle Laboratories, an American defense engineering company, and Kerwin became a senior vice president at Wyle. He retired in 2004.

ALAN BEAN

(b. March 15, 1932, Wheeler, Texas, U.S.)

Alan LaVern Bean was the U.S. astronaut and lunar module pilot on the Apollo 12 mission (November 14–22, 1969), during which two long walks totaling nearly eight hours were made on the Moon's surface. Bean and commander Charles Conrad, Jr., piloted the lunar module *Intrepid* to a pinpoint landing near the unmanned

U.S. spacecraft Surveyor 3, which had landed two years earlier, while astronaut Richard F. Gordon, Jr., orbited overhead in the command module *Yankee Clipper*.

Bean entered the U.S. Navy upon graduation (1955) from the University of Texas, Austin, and served as a test pilot before entering the manned spaceflight program in 1963. In addition to the Apollo 12 mission, Bean was commander of the Skylab 3 mission (July 28–September 25, 1973), during which he, science pilot Owen K. Garriott, and command module pilot Jack Lousma formed the second crew to occupy the orbiting laboratory. The 59 days they spent in space set a new record for the longest spaceflight.

Bean retired from the Navy in 1975 but remained with NASA as chief of the astronaut candidate operations and training group. In 1981 he resigned from NASA to pursue a career as a painter, specializing in subjects drawn from his spaceflight experience.

PAUL J. WEITZ

(b. July 25, 1932, Erie, Pennsylvania, U.S.)

The U.S. astronaut Paul Joseph Weitz made two trips into space. The first was a mission to Skylab in 1973, and the second was a flight of the space shuttle 10 years later.

After graduating from high school Weitz joined the Naval Reserve Officer Training Corps (NROTC) program at Pennsylvania State University, College Station. In 1954 he received a bachelor's degree in aeronautical engineering

Paul Weitz. NASA/Johnson Space Center

and became an officer in the U.S. Navy. In 1956 he became a naval aviator. In 1964 he earned a master's degree from the U.S. Naval Postgraduate School.

Weitz began astronaut training in 1966. He first traveled to space in May 1973 as pilot of the first Skylab mission. The space station Skylab 1 module was placed into orbit unmanned on May 14, and Weitz, Charles Conrad, Jr., and Joseph P. Kerwin followed in an Apollo spacecraft 11 days later. The station had been damaged during the launch, however, and each of the astronauts worked to repair its solar panels and other components. This work included conducting space walks. Once repairs were complete, the three men used the station as a laboratory for scientific experiments. The Skylab mission lasted 28 days and set what was then a new record for the longest manned spaceflight.

Weitz retired from the Navy as a captain in 1976 but remained with NASA. In April 1983 he commanded the first voyage of the space shuttle Challenger. Weitz was an executive at the Lyndon B. Johnson Space Center in Houston, Texas, from 1987 until his retirement in 1994.

WILLIAM A. ANDERS

(b. October 17, 1933, Hong Kong)

The U.S. astronaut William Alison Anders participated in the Apollo 8 flight (December 21–27, 1968), during which the first manned voyage around the Moon was made. The astronauts, including Anders, Frank Borman, and James Lovell, remained in an orbit about 70 miles (112 km) above the surface of the Moon for about 20 hours, transmitting television pictures back to Earth and verifying that lunar landmarks could be used for navigation to lunar landing sites. On one of Apollo 8's orbits of the Moon, Anders took the famous "Earthrise" photograph.

Anders, the son of a U.S. Navy officer, was born in Hong Kong and graduated from the U.S. Naval Academy at Annapolis, Maryland, in 1955. He received a commission in the U.S. Air Force and obtained a master's degree in nuclear engineering from the Air Force Institute of Technology at Wright-Patterson Air Force Base, Dayton, Ohio, in 1962. In 1963 he was selected by NASA in the third group of astronauts.

Apollo 8 was Anders's only spaceflight. Anders resigned from NASA and the Air Force in 1969 to become executive secretary of the National Aeronautics and Space Council. He served as a member of the Atomic Energy Commission (1973–74) and of the Nuclear Regulatory Commission (1974–76); as U.S. ambassador to Norway (1976–77); as general manager of the Nuclear Products Division of General Electric Company (1977–80); as general manager of the Aircraft Equipment Division of General Electric (1980–84); as vice president at Textron (1984–90); and as vice chairman and then chief executive officer at General Dynamics (1990–94).

FRED W. HAISE, JR.

(b. November 14, 1933, Biloxi, Mississippi, U.S.)

The U.S. astronaut Fred Wallace Haise, Jr., participated in the Apollo 13 mission (April 11–17, 1970), in which an intended Moon landing was aborted because of a rupture in a fuel-cell oxygen tank in the service module. The crew, consisting of Haise, John L. Swigert, Jr., and James A. Lovell, Jr., returned safely to Earth, however, making use of the life-support system in the Lunar Module.

Haise became a naval-aviation cadet in 1952 and served as a fighter pilot in the U.S. Marine Corps (1954–56). After obtaining a bachelor's degree (1959) from the University of Oklahoma, Norman, Haise joined NASA as a test pilot; he was selected for the manned space program in 1966.

When the Apollo program was closed in 1977, Haise was assigned to the space shuttle program for two years, after which time he retired from NASA. He then accepted an executive position with the Grumman Aerospace Corporation (later Northrop Grumman Corporation), retiring from the company in 1996.

Fred W. Haise, Jr., 1966. NASA

YURY ALEKSEYEVICH GAGARIN

(b. March 9, 1934, near Gzhatsk, Russia, U.S.S.R. [now
Gagarin, Russia]—d. March 27, 1968, near Moscow)

Yury Alekseyevich Gagarin was a Soviet cosmonaut who in 1961 became the first person to travel into space.

The son of a carpenter on a collective farm, Gagarin graduated as a molder from a trade school near Moscow in 1951. He continued his studies at the industrial college at Saratov and concurrently took a course in flying. On completing this course, he entered the Soviet Air Force cadet school at Orenburg, from which he graduated in 1957.

Gagarin's 4¾-ton Vostok 1 spacecraft was launched at 9:07 AM Moscow time on April 12, 1961, orbited Earth once in 1 hour 29 minutes at a maximum altitude of 187 miles (301 km), and landed at 10:55 AM in the Soviet Union. His spaceflight brought him immediate worldwide fame. He was awarded the Order of Lenin and given the titles of Hero of the Soviet Union and Pilot Cosmonaut of the Soviet Union. Monuments were raised to him, and streets were renamed in his honour across the Soviet Union.

Gagarin never went into space again but took an active part in training other cosmonauts. He made several tours to other nations following his historic flight, and from 1962 he served as a deputy to the Supreme Soviet. Gagarin was killed with another pilot in the crash of a two-seat jet aircraft while on what was described as a routine training flight. His ashes were placed in a niche in the Kremlin wall. After his death in 1968 his hometown of Gzhatsk was renamed Gagarin.

JANE GOODALL

(b. April 3, 1934, London, England)

The British ethologist Dame Jane Goodall (originally called Valerie Jane Morris-Goodall) became internationally known for her exceptionally detailed and long-term research on the chimpanzees of Gombe Stream National Park in Tanzania.

Goodall, who was interested in animal behaviour from an early age, left school at age 18. She worked as a secretary and as a film production assistant until she gained passage to Africa. Once there, Goodall began assisting paleontologist and anthropologist Louis Leakey. Her association with Leakey led eventually to her establishment in June 1960 of a camp in the Gombe Stream Game Reserve (now a national park) so that she could observe the behaviour of chimpanzees in the region. In 1964 she married a Dutch photographer who had been sent in 1962 to Tanzania to film her work (later they divorced). The University of Cambridge in 1965 awarded Goodall a Ph.D. in ethology; she was one of very few candidates to receive a Ph.D. without having first possessed an A.B. degree. Except for short periods of absence, Goodall and her family remained in Gombe until 1975, often directing the fieldwork of other doctoral candidates. In 1977 she cofounded the Jane Goodall Institute for Wildlife Research, Education, and Conservation in California; the centre later moved its headquarters to the Washington, D.C., area.

Over the years Goodall was able to correct a number of misunderstandings about chimpanzees. She found, for example, that the animals are omnivorous, not vegetarian; that they are capable of making and using tools; and, in short, that they have a set of hitherto unrecognized complex and highly developed social behaviours. Goodall wrote a number of books and articles about various aspects of her work, notably *In the Shadow of Man* (1971). She summarized her years of observation in *The Chimpanzees of Gombe: Patterns of Behavior* (1986). Goodall continued to write and lecture about environmental and conservation issues into the early 21st century. The recipient of numerous honours, she was created Dame of the British Empire in 2003.

ALEKSEY ARKHIPOVICH LEONOV

(b. May 30, 1934, near Kemerovo, Russia, U.S.S.R.)

Aleksey Arkhipovich Leonov was a Soviet cosmonaut who was the first person to perform a space walk (i.e., to leave his spacecraft).

After early schooling in Kaliningrad, Leonov joined the Soviet air force in 1953. He completed his flight training in 1957 and served as a fighter pilot until 1959, when he was selected for cosmonaut training.

On March 18, 1965, the Voskhod 2 craft was launched into space with Leonov and Pavel Belyayev aboard. During the second orbit Leonov let himself out of the spacecraft by means of an air lock while about 110 miles (175 km) above the Crimea. Tethered to the ship, Leonov made observations, took motion pictures, and practiced maneuvering in free-fall for about 10 minutes

Three stills from an external movie camera on the Soviet spacecraft Voskhod 2 recording pilot Aleksey Leonov making the first space walk, March 18, 1965. NASA

before reentering Voskhod 2 over western Siberia. The ship landed after completing 17 orbits (26 hours) in space.

A decade later, Leonov was commander of the Soyuz 19 craft that linked in orbit with the U.S. Apollo craft on July 17, 1975, for the first joint Soviet-American spaceflight. He retired as a cosmonaut in 1982, and from 1982 to 1991 he worked at the Yury Gagarin Cosmonaut Training Centre in Star City, near Moscow. In 2004 he wrote a book, *Two Sides of the Moon: Our Story of the Cold War Space Race*, with American astronaut David Scott.

VALERY BYKOVSKY

(b. August 2, 1934, Pavlovsky Posad,
Russia, U.S.S.R.)

The Soviet cosmonaut Valery Fyodorovich Bykovsky orbited Earth 81 times in the spacecraft Vostok 5, from June 14 to 19, 1963.

Bykovsky started flying lessons at the age of 16, joined the army in 1952, and in 1959 became a jet fighter pilot. In 1960 he began his training as a cosmonaut at the Zhukovsky Military Engineering Academy.

On June 16, 1963, after Bykovsky had been in orbit two days, the Soviet Union launched Vostok 6, carrying Valentina Tereshkova, the first woman to travel in space. The two ships held parallel orbits, at one point approaching to within 3 miles (5 km) of one another, but did not rendezvous. They returned to Earth three hours apart.

Bykovsky had spent nearly five days in orbit, which is the record for the longest solo spaceflight.

Bykovsky was made a member of the Communist Party on June 18, while still in orbit, and after his return he received his country's highest honour, Hero of the Soviet Union. He was one of the few men to receive the Soviet Union's highest combat award during peacetime, the Order of the Red Star, presumably for air-combat action in a border incident.

He was chief of cosmonaut training for the Apollo-Soyuz Test Project, which was carried out in July 1975, and was command pilot of Soyuz 22, a 190-hour flight that began on September 15, 1976. Bykovsky was commander of Soyuz 31, which lifted off with East German cosmonaut Sigmund Jähn aboard on August 26, 1978. On the space station Salyut 6, he and Jähn conducted scientific experiments before returning to Earth on Soyuz 29 on September 3, 1978. Bykovsky left the cosmonaut program in 1988 and was director of the House of Soviet Science and Culture in Berlin until 1990.

MAXIE ANDERSON

(b. September 10, 1934, Sayre, Oklahoma, U.S.—d. June 27, 1983, near Bad Brückenau, West Germany [now in Germany])

Max Leroy ("Maxie") Anderson was an American balloonist who, with Ben Abruzzo and Larry Newman, made the first transatlantic balloon flight and, with his son Kristian, made the first nonstop trans-North American balloon flight.

Anderson entered the Missouri Military Academy, Mexico, Missouri, at the age of eight and throughout his schooling worked summers with his father, a pipeline builder. Anderson held a pilot's license at the age of 15, having lied about his age. By the age of 29 he owned his own mining company in Albuquerque, New Mexico. He began flying hot-air balloons in New Mexico, alone and with his friend Ben Abruzzo, who was also a light-aircraft flyer (planes, gliders, and helicopters).

Maxie Anderson (centre), flanked by Ben Abruzzo (left) and Larry Newman, after the trio had successfully crossed the Atlantic Ocean in a hot air balloon in 1978. Keystone/Hulton Archive/Getty Images

In 1977, Anderson and Abruzzo decided to attempt the transatlantic flight in honour of the 50th anniversary of Charles Lindbergh's pioneering flight from New York to Paris. Ed Yost, a balloonist and balloon builder whose transatlantic flight had failed in 1958, built the *Double Eagle*, a helium balloon, for them and trained them to fly it. They launched the balloon near Marshfield, Massachusetts, on September 9, 1977, but had to set down off the coast of Iceland on September 13. In 1978 a third crew member was added, Larry Newman, head of the Electra Flyer Corporation, a maker of hang gliders, who applied his expertise to the building of the *Double Eagle* II. On August 11 it was launched from Presque Isle, Maine, and landed near Miserey, France, on August 17.

On May 8, 1980, Anderson and his son Kristian launched the helium balloon Kitty Hawk from Fort Baker, California, and landed, on May 12, at Sainte-Félicité, Quebec, Canada, the first trans-North American nonstop balloon flight. Three years later, Anderson was killed in an accident during a balloon race.

SIR WALLY HERBERT

(b. October 24, 1934, York, England—d. June 12, 2007, Inverness, Scotland)

British polar explorer Sir Walter William Herbert led the British Transarctic Expedition (1968–69) that crossed the Arctic Ocean via the North Pole on an epic

15-month trek from Point Barrow, Alaska, to Spitsbergen in Norway's Svalbard archipelago.

Herbert spent several years trekking in Antarctica in the 1950s and early '60s, first with the Falkland Islands Dependencies Survey and then with teams from New Zealand. On February 21, 1968, Herbert and three colleagues, each with a sled and team of dogs, left Point Barrow. They reached the Pole on April 6, 1969. By the time the team reached Spitsbergen on May 29, they had walked more than 3,600 miles (5,800 km) and had taken some 250 ice-core samples. In later years he lived with his family in Greenland, where he made an unsuccessful attempt in 1979 to circumnavigate the island. His books included *Across the Top of the World* (1969) and *The Noose of Laurels* (1989), in which he determined that American explorer Robert Peary, famed for being the first man to reach the North Pole, had actually fallen short in his attempt. Herbert was knighted in 2000.

ROGER B. CHAFFEE

(b. February 15, 1935, Grand Rapids, Michigan, U.S.—d. January 27, 1967, Cape Kennedy, Florida)

U.S. astronaut Roger Bruce Chaffee was a member of the three-man Apollo 1 crew killed when a flash fire swept through their space capsule during a simulation of a launching scheduled for February 21, 1967. Chaffee died along with the veteran space travelers Virgil I. Grissom and Edward H. White II. They were the first casualties of the U.S. space program.

After earning his B.S. in aeronautical engineering from Purdue University, West Lafayette, Indiana, in 1957, Chaffee became a Navy pilot. He was chosen as one of the third group of astronauts in 1963.

SYLVIA ALICE EARLE

(b. August 30, 1935, Gibbstown, New Jersey, U.S.)

American oceanographer and explorer Sylvia Alice Earle became known for her research on marine algae and her books and documentaries designed to raise awareness of the threats that overfishing and pollution pose to the world's oceans. A pioneer in the use of modern self-contained underwater breathing apparatus (SCUBA) gear and the development of deep-sea submersibles, Earle also held the world record for the deepest untethered dive.

Earle was the second of three children born to electrical engineer Lewis Reade Earle and his wife, Alice Freas Richie. She spent her early life on a small farm near Camden, New Jersey, where she gained a respect and appreciation for the wonders of nature through her own explorations of nearby woods and the empathy her parents showed to living things. When she was 12, her father moved the family to Dunedin, Florida, where the family's waterfront property afforded Earle the opportunity to investigate living things inhabiting nearby salt marshes and sea grass beds.

Earle first learned to dive with scuba gear while attending Florida State University, Tallahassee. She majored in botany and graduated in 1955. Later that year she enrolled in the master's program in botany at Duke University, Durham, North Carolina, graduating in 1956. She completed her thesis work on algae in the Gulf of Mexico. Earle married American zoologist John Taylor in 1957 and started a family. (She and Taylor later divorced.) She completed a Ph.D. in 1966, publishing her dissertation *Phaeophyta of the Eastern Gulf of Mexico* in 1969. For this project she collected more than 20,000 samples of algae.

Earle's postgraduate experiences were a mixture of research and groundbreaking oceanographic exploration. In 1965 she accepted a position as the resident director of Cape Haze Marine Laboratories in Sarasota, Florida.

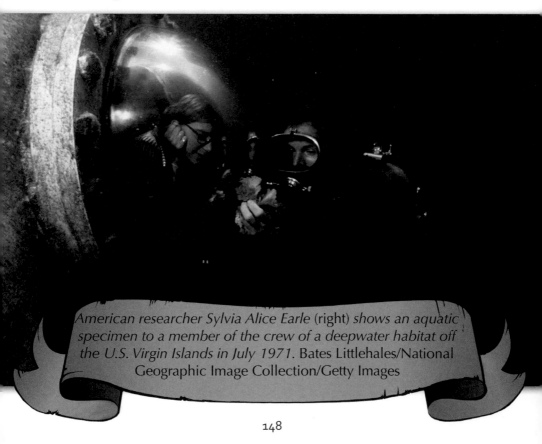

American researcher Sylvia Alice Earle (right) *shows an aquatic specimen to a member of the crew of a deepwater habitat off the U.S. Virgin Islands in July 1971.* Bates Littlehales/National Geographic Image Collection/Getty Images

In 1967 she became a research fellow at the Farlow Herbarium of Harvard University and a research scholar at the Radcliffe Institute. In 1968 she discovered undersea dunes off the coast of the Bahamas. In 1970 she led the first all-female team of women aquanauts as part of the Tektite II experiment, a project designed to explore the marine realm and test the viability of deepwater habitats and the health effects of prolonged living in underwater structures. The habitat was located about 50 feet (15 metres) below the surface of Great Lameshur Bay off the island of St. John in the U.S. Virgin Islands. During the two-week experiment, she observed the effects of pollution on coral reefs first hand. Occurring during a time when American women were just beginning to enter fields traditionally staffed by men, the Tektite II project captured the imagination of scientists and nonscientists alike because Earle's team did the same work as previous all-male crews.

Earle led numerous undersea expeditions over her career. Her oceanographic research took her to such places as the Galapagos Islands, China, and the Bahamas. In the 1970s she began an association with the National Geographic Society to produce books and films on life in Earth's oceans. In 1976 she became a curator and a research biologist at the California Academy of Sciences, San Francisco. In 1979 she became curator of phycology at the California Academy of Sciences. On September 19, 1979, she set the world untethered diving record, descending 1,250 feet (381 metres) beneath the surface of the Pacific Ocean in a JIM diving suit, a special diving apparatus that maintains an interior pressure of 1 standard atmosphere (14.70 pounds per square inch [1.03 kg per square cm]). During the early 1980s Earle founded Deep Ocean Engineering and Deep Ocean Technology with British engineer Graham Hawkes, her third husband. Together they designed the submersible *Deep Rover*, a vehicle capable of reaching depths of some 3,000 feet (900 metres) beneath the surface of the ocean.

Earle served on the National Advisory Committee on Oceans and Atmosphere between 1980 and 1984. Between 1990 and 1992 Earle was the chief scientist at the National Oceanic and Atmospheric Administration (NOAA), the first woman to serve in that position. In 1998 she became the National Geographic Society's first female explorer in residence. Throughout her career she published more than 100 scientific papers. Her other works include *Sea Change: A Message of the Oceans* (1994), *Wild Ocean: America's Parks Under the Sea* (1999) with American author Wolcott Henry, and *The World Is Blue: How Our Fate and the Ocean's Are One* (2009).

GHERMAN STEPANOVICH TITOV

(b. September 11, 1935, Verkhneye Zhilino, near Barnaul, Russia, U.S.S.R.—d. September 20, 2000, Moscow)

G herman Stepanovich Titov was the Soviet cosmonaut who piloted the Vostok 2 spacecraft, launched on August 6, 1961, on the first manned spaceflight of more than a single orbit; Yury Gagarin had made the first orbit of Earth on April 12, 1961.

Titov was accepted in 1953 for aviation cadet training, graduating in 1957 as a jet fighter pilot from the Stalingrad Flying Academy. In 1960 he entered cosmonaut training, during the course of which he received the Order of Lenin for an engineering proposal and was selected as the back-up cosmonaut to Gagarin for Vostok 1.

During the Vostok 2 flight of 25 hours 18 minutes, Titov was assigned the communications code name Eagle. His radio identification, "I am Eagle!," was spoken with intense excitement and made an impression on listeners around the world. Following his flight Titov was named a Hero of the Soviet Union and received another Order of Lenin. In 1962 he became a deputy of the Supreme Soviet, a position that he held until 1970, and in 1968 he graduated from the Zhukovsky Air Force Engineering Academy. Titov became a major general in 1975. In subsequent years he worked as an assistant to the chief editor of the *Journal of Aviation and Cosmonautics*. Following the dissolution of the Soviet Union in 1991, Titov entered politics and was elected to the Duma, the lower house of the Russian parliament, in 1995; he did not run for a second term in 1999. His writings in English translation include *I Am Eagle* (1962) and *Seventeen Cosmic Dawns* (1963).

SIGMUND JÄHN

(b. February 13, 1937, Morgenröthe-Rautenkranz, Vogtland, Germany)

Sigmund Jähn was an East German cosmonaut who became the first German in space.

As a young man Jähn trained to become a printer, but in 1955 he joined the East German air force, where he became a pilot and a military scientist. In 1966 he left East Germany to study at the Gagarin Military Air Academy in the Soviet Union. Upon completing his studies, he worked in pilot education and flight safety and applied his fluency in Russian to translating a number of Soviet military and political publications into German.

In 1976 Jähn was selected to train as the first cosmonaut in the Soviet Intercosmos program. This program placed non-Soviet cosmonauts on routine flights with experienced Soviet cosmonauts in a campaign to demonstrate Soviet solidarity with Warsaw Pact states and other sympathetic countries. On August 26, 1978, Jähn lifted off with Soviet cosmonaut Valery Bykovsky aboard Soyuz 31. On the space station Salyut, he conducted scientific experiments before returning to Earth on Soyuz 29 on September 3, 1978.

Following the Intercosmos mission, Jähn was named a Hero of the Soviet Union and awarded the Order of Lenin, the Soviet Union's highest civilian honour. His home country of East Germany elevated him to a kind of socialist folk hero and proclaimed proudly that the first German in space had been not a West German but an East German citizen. In 1983 Jähn earned a Ph.D. in geophysics from the Central Institute for Physics of the Earth, at Potsdam. After the reunification of Germany, he represented the country and the European Space Agency as a consultant at the Yury Gagarin Cosmonaut Training Centre in Star City, Russia.

VALENTINA TERESHKOVA

(b. March 6, 1937, Maslennikovo,
Russia, U.S.S.R.)

Soviet cosmonaut Valentina Vladimirovna Tereshkova became, in 1963, the first woman to travel into space.

Although she had no pilot training, Tereshkova was an accomplished amateur parachutist and on this basis was accepted for the cosmonaut program when she volunteered in 1961. On June 16, 1963, she was launched in the spacecraft Vostok 6, which completed 48 orbits in 71 hours. In space at the same time was Valery F. Bykovsky, who had been launched two days earlier in Vostok 5; both landed on June 19. She left the program just after her flight, and on November 3, 1963, she was married to Andriyan G. Nikolayev, another cosmonaut.

From 1966 until 1991 Tereshkova was an active member in the U.S.S.R. Supreme Soviet. She directed the Soviet Women's Committee in 1968, and from 1974 to 1991 she served as a member of the Supreme Soviet Presidium. In 2008 she became the deputy chair of the parliament of Yaroslavl province as a member of the United Russia party. Tereshkova was named a Hero of the Soviet Union and was twice awarded the Order of Lenin.

ROBERT LAUREL CRIPPEN

(b. September 11, 1937, Beaumont, Texas, U.S.)

The U.S. astronaut Robert Laurel Crippen served as pilot on the first U.S. space shuttle orbital flight.

Crippen graduated from the University of Texas, Austin, with a degree in aerospace engineering in 1960. He entered the U.S. Air Force Manned Orbiting Laboratory program in 1966 and transferred to NASA's astronaut corps in 1969. He was named commander of the Skylab Medical Experiments Altitude Test several years later and was a member of the support crews for Skylab 2, 3, and 4 and the Apollo-Soyuz Test Project.

Manned by Crippen and John W. Young, the shuttle *Columbia*, the world's first reusable spacecraft, was launched on April 12, 1981. The two astronauts landed the airplanelike craft on April 14, after having orbited Earth 36 times. Crippen later commanded the second flight of the space shuttle *Challenger*. This flight (June 18–24, 1983) included the first American woman in space, Sally Ride, and made Crippen the first to fly in two shuttle missions.

In 1984 he commanded two more shuttle flights. STS-41-C (*Challenger*, April 6–13, 1984) was the first mission in which a satellite, the malfunctioning Solar Maximum Mission, was repaired in Earth orbit. He then commanded STS-41-G (*Challenger*, October 5–13, 1984), which was the first spaceflight with a seven-person crew and during which astronaut Kathryn Sullivan became the first American woman to walk in space.

From 1984 Crippen was a NASA administrator, during which time he was director of the space shuttle program (1990–92) and then director of the Kennedy Space Center in Florida (1992–95). After leaving the space program, he worked in private aerospace companies until retiring in 2001.

VALERY VLADIMIROVICH POLYAKOV

(b. April 27, 1942, Tula, Russia, U.S.S.R.)

The Russian cosmonaut Valery Vladimirovich Polyakov holds the record for the longest single spaceflight in history.

Polyakov had an early interest in spaceflight, and in 1971 he joined the Institute of Biomedical Problems in Moscow, the leading Soviet institution for space biomedicine. In 1972 he passed his exams to become one of the first doctor-cosmonaut trainees from the institute. He earned a Candidate of Medical Sciences degree in 1976.

After serving as reserve cosmonaut for several crews, Polyakov flew his first mission into space in 1988–89 as the doctor-cosmonaut on board Soyuz TM-6. During his 241-day flight aboard the Mir space station, he conducted numerous medical experiments.

After his mission, Polyakov returned to administrative duties before training for a second mission. He flew as doctor-cosmonaut of Soyuz TM-18 to the Mir space station in 1994. It was during this stay on Mir—from January 8, 1994, to March 22, 1995—that he set the record of 438 days for the longest continuous stay in space.

In 1995 Polyakov formally retired as a cosmonaut, although he retained his duties as deputy director of the Institute for Biomedical Problems, a post to which he had been appointed in 1989. He simultaneously served as deputy chair of the commission in charge of certifying Russian cosmonauts.

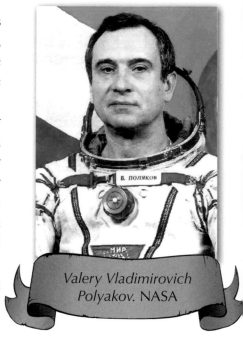

Valery Vladimirovich Polyakov. NASA

PYOTR ILYICH KLIMUK

(b. July 10, 1942, Komarovka, Belorussia,
U.S.S.R. [now Belarus])

The Soviet cosmonaut Pyotr Ilyich Klimuk flew three times in space. He later was an official at the Yury Gagarin Cosmonaut Training Centre near Moscow.

Klimuk became a cosmonaut trainee in 1965, at age 23. Between 1967 and 1969 he trained for a flight around the Moon that was eventually canceled. He flew his first mission into space in 1973 as commander of Soyuz 13, during which he and his crewmate Valentin Lebedev spent a week in Earth orbit. Having transferred into space station training, Klimuk flew his second spaceflight in 1975 as commander of Soyuz 18, a 63-day flight to the Salyut 4 space station. At the time, this was the longest Soviet spaceflight. He ended his career with a third mission in 1978, as commander of Soyuz 30, during which a Polish cosmonaut, Mirosław Hermaszewski, accompanied him on a short visit to the Salyut 6 space station.

Klimuk officially resigned as a cosmonaut in 1982. From 1982 to 1991 he headed the political department at the Yury Gagarin Cosmonaut Training Centre. After the dissolution of the Soviet Union, in September 1991, he was selected to head the centre, a position that he held until 2003. After his retirement, Klimuk served as an adviser to the president of Belarus. He was twice named Hero of the Soviet Union (1973, 1975).

Soviet cosmonaut Pyotr Klimuk. www.spacefacts.de

AKIYAMA TOYOHIRO

(b. July 22, 1942, Tokyo, Japan)

The Japanese journalist and television reporter Akiyama Toyohiro became, in 1990, the first Japanese citizen and the first journalist to travel into space. Akiyama was also the first fare-paying civilian passenger (non-professional astronaut) to participate in a spaceflight.

Akiyama earned his bachelor's degree at the International Christian University in Mitaka, Tokyo. In 1966 he joined the Tokyo Broadcasting System (TBS), a Japanese television company, as a reporter. After working for the British Broadcasting Corporation World Service in London for four years (1967–71), he was transferred to the TBS Division of Foreign News and eventually served as the chief TBS correspondent in Washington, D.C., for four years (1984–88). In August 1989 Akiyama was selected for cosmonaut training for a commercial flight to the Soviet Mir space station. His journey was sponsored by TBS. The exact terms of the deal were not revealed, but the Soviets claimed to have received $14 million (other estimates are in the range of $10–$12 million), and the total expense of the trip and the ensuing broadcast for TBS is thought to have exceeded $20 million. It was the first commercial spaceflight in history.

Akiyama completed the cosmonaut training course at the Yury Gagarin Cosmonaut Training Centre in Star City, Russia, and flew into space aboard Soyuz TM-11 on December 2, 1990. The mission, named Mir Kosmoreporter, lasted eight days, and Akiyama landed back on Earth on Soyuz TM-10 on December 10. During the mission, Akiyama made daily television broadcasts for TBS, conducting live reports from the Mir space station.

After completing his spaceflight, Akiyama returned to TBS and eventually served as the deputy director of the TBS News Division. He retired from TBS in 1995 to pursue organic farming in Fukushima prefecture. In March 2011, in the wake of the nuclear accident triggered by the earthquake and tsunami there, Akiyama was forced to evacuate and then abandon his farm. He later took a faculty position at the Kyoto University of Art and Design.

Akiyama Toyohiro. www.space-facts.de

CHARLES ROBERT BURTON

(b. December 13, 1942, Cape Town, South Africa—d. July 15, 2002, Framfield, East Sussex, England)

The South African-born British explorer Charles Robert Burton was part of the first team to circumnavigate the globe from pole to pole along a meridian. The Transglobe Expedition, led by Sir Ranulph Fiennes and funded by Charles, prince of Wales, departed from Greenwich, England, on September 2, 1979, and returned there on August 29, 1982. During their roughly 52,000-mile (84,000-km) expedition, the explorers survived a polar bear attack, the loss of crucial supplies, and three months of being marooned on a drifting ice floe. Upon his return, Burton was awarded the Polar Medal. He later entered the private securities trade.

SIR RANULPH FIENNES

(b. March 7, 1944, Windsor, Berkshire, England)

Sir Ranulph Twisleton-Wykeham-Fiennes, 3rd Baronet (popularly called Ran), is a British adventurer, pioneering polar explorer, and writer, who, among his many exploits, in 1979–82 led the first north-south surface circumnavigation of the world (i.e., along a meridian).

Fiennes inherited the baronetcy at birth, as his father, an army officer, had already died in action during World War II. His family moved to his paternal grandmother's home in South Africa in early 1947 and returned to England in 1954. He entered Eton College at age 13 but left after three generally unhappy years with marks insufficient for admission into the Royal Military Academy at Sandhurst. His goal had been to become an officer in the Royal Scots Greys, the regiment that his father had commanded during the war. He was able to secure a commission to the regiment by attending another military academy and served in the unit until he was accepted for training by the Special Air Service (SAS), the elite British fighting unit. He was still in training with the SAS when he was dismissed in 1966, however, for attempting to destroy part of a movie set in the Cotswolds being used to film *Dr. Doolittle* (he objected to the filmmakers' damming of a creek). He spent most of the remainder of his military career in Oman fighting for the sultan there against Marxist insurgents.

In 1969 Fiennes led his first expedition: a journey by hovercraft up the White Nile River that began in eastern Sudan and ended at Lake Victoria in southern Uganda. The following year he left the military and married Virginia ("Ginny") Pepper, whom he had met as a child and who, until her death in 2004, would be the collaborator on many of his subsequent expeditions and adventures. A trip to Jostedals Glacier in Norway (1970) was followed by the first north-south traverse of British Columbia, Canada, via water (1971) and by a northward trek into the Arctic (1977) in preparation for his circumpolar expedition.

Preparation for what came to be called the Transglobe Expedition began in 1972 and occupied much of Fiennes's and Ginny's time during the rest of the decade. The trekking team, led by Fiennes and including fellow Britons Charles Burton and Oliver Shepard, had a support crew of some three dozen people, including Ginny. They departed from Greenwich, England, on September 12, 1979, attempting to stay as close as possible to the Greenwich meridian as they journeyed southward over land and water, until they reached the coast of Antarctica in January 1980. They remained there until October, when Fiennes, Burton, and Shepherd departed on snowmobiles for the South Pole, which they reached on December 15. Setting out again after a short time at the American base there, they arrived at the Scott Base on the west coast of Antarctica in mid-January 1981, having made the continental traverse in a record-setting 67 days.

There they were met by their support ship, the *Benjamin Bowring*, and the rest of their team, and over the next several months they undertook a series of sea voyages northward through the Pacific Ocean, arriving at the Yukon River delta in western Alaska at the end of June. In July and August Fiennes and Burton (Shepard had by then left the expedition) headed east and north in an open boat through the Northwest Passage to Ellesmere Island in Nunavut, Canada, before proceeding on foot in September to the settlement of Alert on the island's north shore. After wintering there for five months, the pair set out for the North Pole in mid-February 1982, arriving there on April 11 after an arduous trek by snowmobile and sledge. The journey home was no less challenging, hampered by difficult ice conditions and stretches of open water. After the two spent more than three months on a drifting ice floe, the *Benjamin Bowring* was able to retrieve them and sail home to Britain. The expedition arrived back in Greenwich on August 29, nearly three years to the day after they had departed and after having traveled some 52,000 miles (84,000 km).

Remarkable as the transpolar journey had been, Fiennes subsequently undertook similar pioneering and challenging adventures. Between 1986 and 1990 he and the British physician and adventurer Mike Stroud made several unsuccessful attempts to reach the North Pole unsupported (i.e., without outside contact or resupply) and on foot before deciding to try the same feat in

Antarctica in 1992–93. They did cross the continent—in the process setting a distance record for unsupported polar treks—but they were forced to abandon their quest just short of the opposite shore. Fiennes attempted one more polar feat: a solo unsupported hike to the North Pole that he had to abort after falling through the ice and getting severe frostbite on his hands that eventually necessitated amputating portions of fingers on his left hand.

In addition to his polar exploits, Fiennes pursued other adventures. Among the most notable was an expedition that in 1991 discovered the ancient trading city of Ubar in Oman. For sheer audac-ity, however, perhaps nothing

British explorers Ranulph Fiennes (left) and Anton Bowring discuss-ing a charity trek across Antarctica in the winter of 2013. Fiennes later had to drop out of the expedition due to frostbite. Alexander Joe/AFP/ Getty Images

topped his running (with Stroud) seven marathons on seven continents in seven consecutive days in 2003—though the "Antarctic" race was actually in the Falkland Islands—a feat he accomplished some four months after suffering a heart attack and undergoing bypass surgery. In addition, in 2009 Fiennes became the oldest Briton to successfully climb Mount Everest, after he twice (in 2005 and 2008) had to turn back short of the summit because of his heart condition (he actually had a heart attack while on the mountain in 2005).

Fiennes was a prolific writer. Most of his books were concerned with his exploits and adventures — e.g., *To the Ends of the Earth* (1983), about the Transglobe Expedition, and Atlantis of the Sands (1992), on the search for Ubar. Others, however, focused on topics of interest to him, including *The Feather Men* (1991), about an alleged plot by members of the SAS to thwart a series of assassinations by Middle Eastern terrorists, and a best-selling biography of Robert Falcon Scott that was published in 2003. He also wrote two volumes of autobiography, *Living Dangerously* (1987) and *Mad, Bad & Dangerous to Know* (2007), as well as *Fit for Life* (1998), a self-help book. Among the numerous honours he received were the Order of the British Empire (OBE) in 1993 and the Polar Medal in 1984 (recognized again in 1995 for his work in both polar regions) Many of the endeavours undertaken by Fiennes were fund-raisers, and over the years he raised millions for a variety of charities.

STEVE FOSSETT

(b. April 22, 1944, Jackson, Tennessee, U.S.—
disappeared September 3, 2007, western
Nevada)

James Stephen Fossett was an American businessman and adventurer who set a number of world records, most notably in aviation and sailing. In 2002 he became the first balloonist to circumnavigate the world alone, and in 2005 he completed the first nonstop, solo global flight in an airplane.

Fossett grew up in California, where he studied economics and philosophy at Stanford University, Palo Alto (B.A., 1966). After earning an M.B.A. (1968) at Washington University in St. Louis, Missouri, he became a successful commodities broker, and in 1980 he founded the securities company Lakota Trading. Fossett undertook a number of challenges, including swimming the English Channel (1985), before gaining international attention with his ballooning feats. In 1995 he registered his first record in the sport with a solo transpacific flight. The following year he began his highly publicized effort to become the first person to balloon around the world alone. The initial attempt, however, ended after three days, and a series of subsequent efforts also failed. In 2002 Fossett made his sixth attempt at the record, taking off from Northam, Western Australia, in the *Spirit of Freedom* and drifting eastward. On July 2 he made history as he crossed his starting point, eventually landing in the outback of Queensland.

In 2005 Fossett became the first person to fly an airplane around the world solo without stopping or refueling. Piloting the *GlobalFlyer*, a specialized plane that featured 13 fuel tanks and a 7-foot (2-metre) cockpit, he took off from Salinas, Kansas, on February 28 and returned there some 67 hours later, on March 3. On February 8, 2006, he undertook the longest nonstop airplane flight, taking off from Cape Canaveral, Florida, aboard the *GlobalFlyer*. Some 76 hours later, on February 11, he made an emergency landing in Bournemouth, England, having covered a record 26,389.3 miles (42,469.5 km).

Fossett was also renowned as a speed sailor. In 2001 he and his crew recorded the quickest west-to-east transatlantic crossing—4 days, 17 hours, 28 minutes, 6 seconds—and in 2004 he circumnavigated the globe in

Entrepreneur and adventurer Steve Fossett greets the crowd gathered in Salina, Kansas, after he completed the first solo, nonstop flight around the world without refueling. Carl De Souza/AFP/Getty Images

an unprecedented time of 58 days, 9 hours, 32 minutes, 45 seconds. During his lifetime he set some 100 records in sailing and aviation, all of which later were broken. His other achievements included the fastest flight (742.02 miles [1,194.17 km] per hour) in a nonsupersonic airplane (2001) as well as a number of gliding records.

On September 3, 2007, Fossett was reported missing after his single-engine plane disappeared during a scouting mission in western Nevada. Subsequent search efforts were hampered by the area's remoteness and rugged terrain. On

February 15, 2008, Fossett was declared dead by a court in Chicago. In October the wreckage of his plane and what were believed to be his remains were found in Inyo National Forest, Nevada; DNA tests later confirmed that the bones were those of Fossett.

REINHOLD MESSNER

(b. September 17, 1944, Bressanone [Brixon], Italy)

The Italian mountain climber and polar trekker Reinhold Messner was renowned for his pioneering and difficult ascents of the world's highest peaks. In 1978 he and Austrian Peter Habeler were the first to climb Mount Everest (29,035 feet [8,850 metres]), the highest mountain in the world, without the use of contained oxygen for breathing, and two years later he completed the first solo ascent of Everest, also without supplemental oxygen. He was the first person to climb all 14 of the world's mountains that exceed an elevation of 26,250 feet (8,000 metres).

Messner was raised in a German-speaking region of the Dolomite Alps of northern Italy. His father introduced him to mountaineering, and from the age of 13 he made numerous difficult climbs, first on mountains in the Eastern Alps and later on other Alpine peaks. During the 1960s Messner became one of the earliest and strongest proponents of what came to be called the "Alpine" style of mountaineering, which advocates the use of minimal amounts of lightweight equipment and little or no out-side support (e.g., the Sherpa porters typically employed in the Himalayas). He was joined in this philosophy by his younger brother Günther and by Habeler, whom Messner met on an expedition to the Peruvian Andes in 1969.

He made his first trip to the Himalayas in 1970, when he and Günther scaled Nanga Parbat (26,660 feet [8,126 metres]) and were the first to ascend by way of its Rupal (south) face; his brother died during the descent, and Reinhold barely survived the ordeal, losing several toes to frostbite. In 1975 Messner and Habeler made their first Alpine-style ascent of an 8,000-metre mountain without supplemental oxygen when they climbed the northwest-ern face of Gasherbrum I (Hidden Peak; 26,470 feet [8,068 metres]) in the Karakoram Range.

For their historic oxygen-free climb of Mount Everest in 1978, Messner and Habeler accompanied a large German-Austrian conventional (i.e., Sherpa-supported) expedition to the mountain. Setting out on their own from about 26,200 feet (7,985 metres) on the morning of May 8, the two reached the summit in the early after-noon. Habeler, fearing the effects of oxygen deprivation, descended quickly, with Messner following more slowly. Messner recounted the adventure in *Everest: Expedition zum Endpunkt* (1978; *Everest: Expedition to the Ultimate*, 1979). Messner's landmark solo ascent of Everest in 1980 was equally remarkable. After three days of exhaust-ing climbing on the north side of the mountain (which included a fall into a crevasse), on August 20 he stood on the summit. As he described it later,

> *I was in continual agony; I have never in my whole life been so tired as on the summit of Everest that day. I just sat and sat there, oblivious to everything....I knew I was physically at the end of my tether.*

Messner continued tackling lofty peaks, usually by untried routes. In 1978 he had again climbed Nanga Parbat, reaching the summit alone by a new route, and in 1979 he had led a team of six to the top of K2 (28,251 feet [8,611 metres]), the world's second highest mountain. In 1983 he led a party on a notable ascent of Cho Oyu (26,906 feet [8,201 metres]) using a new approach, the southwest face, and the following year made the first traverse between two 26,250-foot (8,000-metre) peaks: Gasherbrum I and II. By 1986 he had climbed all of the world's 26,250-foot (8,000-metre) mountains, many of them twice.

In 1989–90 Messner and German Arved Fuchs became the first people to traverse Antarctica via the South Pole by foot without either animals or machines. Their journey, which covered some 1,740 miles (2,800 km), was accomplished in 92 days. Another notable adventure was Messner's 1,250-mile (2,000-km) solo trek across the Gobi (desert) in Mongolia in 2004. He also established a series of mountain-themed museums in the Alps of northern Italy, beginning with one near Bolzano in 2006. Messner served one term (1999–2004) in the European Parliament in 1999, where he mainly championed environmental issues.

Messner was the author of several dozen books in German, several of which were translated into English. Notable among these are his autobiography, *Die Freiheit, aufzubrechen, wohin ich will: ein Bergsteigerleben* (1989; Eng. trans. *Free Spirit: A Climber's Life*, 1991); *Antarktis: Himmel und Hölle zugleich* (1990; *Antarctica: Both Heaven and Hell*, 1992), describing his trek across Antarctica; and *Der nackte Berg* (2002; *The Naked Mountain*, 2003), about his fateful climb of Nanga Parbat in 1970.

BRIAN JONES

(b. March 27, 1947, Bristol, England)

The British aviator Brian Jones completed—with captain Bertrand Piccard—the first nonstop circumnavigation of the globe by balloon on March 20, 1999. The trip, begun by Jones and Piccard on March 1 aboard the *Breitling Orbiter 3*, took 19 days, 21 hours, and 55 minutes to complete. Starting in the Swiss Alps, the balloon carried the pair over Europe, Africa, Asia, Central America, and the Pacific and Atlantic oceans.

Jones learned to fly at age 16 and left school early for a 13-year stint in the Royal Air Force. Although he did not get involved in ballooning until 1986, by 1989 he had acquired a balloon-flying license and had become an instructor. He served as project manager of a number of *Breitling* missions, overseeing construction of the craft. He was originally designated as a third copilot of *Breitling Orbiter 3* but became

Brian Jones, 1999. Breitling SA

Piccard's sole copilot after Wim Verstraeten and another pilot backed out of the flight.

Several high-profile attempts to circumnavigate the globe via balloon, including those by American adventurer Steve Fossett and British billionaire Richard Branson, failed in the months leading up to Piccard and Jones's successful flight. Although Piccard and Jones had to skirt a number of no-fly zones, they received permission to fly over southern China and thus were able to catch a key jet stream air current over the Pacific. They ended their historic flight on March 21 in Egypt, with a safe landing near the Pyramids of Giza. The *Breitling Orbiter 3* gondola was recovered and placed on display at the Smithsonian Institution's National Air and Space Museum in Washington, D.C.

Upon completion of the circumnavigation, Jones helped plan a number of high-profile ballooning projects, including an attempt to break the ballooning altitude record. In 2004 he joined Piccard's Solar Impulse project (the design, construction, and flying of a wholly solar-powered airplane) as a mission coordinator. He was named an Officer of the Order of the British Empire (OBE) in 1999.

SVETLANA YEVGENYEVNA SAVITSKAYA

(b. August 8, 1948, Moscow, Russia, U.S.S.R.)

The Soviet cosmonaut Svetlana Yevgenyevna Savitskaya became, in 1984, the first woman to walk in space.

The daughter of World War II fighter ace Yevgeny Savitsky, Savitskaya showed an aptitude for aviation at an early age. By her 22nd birthday, she had recorded more than 400 parachute jumps and had claimed the top spot at the World Aerobatic Championships. She earned an engineering degree from Moscow Aviation Institute in 1972 and was accepted as a test pilot candidate. She ultimately qualified to fly more than 20 different types of aircraft, earning a number of women's speed and altitude records in the process.

In 1980 Savitskaya was selected to join the Soviet space program, and she began training for work with Soyuz and Salyut spacecraft. On August 19, 1982, as part of the Soyuz T-7 mission to the Salyut 7 space station, she became the second woman to enter outer space. On her second trip to Salyut 7, she became the first woman to perform a space walk when, on July 25, 1984, she participated in welding experiments on the outer hull of the space station.

Savitskaya returned to Earth and took an executive position at the aerospace design bureau Energia. She made the transition to politics, and in 1989 she was elected to the Duma as a member of the Communist Party. She remained active in the Duma throughout the dissolution of the Soviet Union and the

Svetlana Yevgenyevna Savitskaya.
www.spacefacts.de

establishment of Russia in the 1990s, and by 2003 she had risen to the fourth highest position in the Communist Party's ranks. She served as the deputy chairperson for the Duma's defense committee and won reelection to her seat in 2007 and 2011.

CHRISTA CORRIGAN MCAULIFFE

(b. September 2, 1948, Boston, Massachusetts, U.S.—d. January 28, 1986, in-flight, off Cape Canaveral, Florida)

Sharon Christa Corrigan McAuliffe was an American teacher who was chosen to be the first private citizen in space. The deaths of McAuliffe and her fellow crew members in the 1986 space shuttle *Challenger* disaster were deeply felt by the country and had a strong effect on the U.S. space program.

Christa Corrigan earned a B.A. from Framingham (Massachusetts) State College in 1970 and the same year married Steve McAuliffe. She received an M.A. in education from Bowie (Maryland) State College (now University) in 1978. In 1970 she began a teaching career that impressed both her colleagues and her students with her energy and dedication.

When in 1984 some 10,000 applications were processed to determine who would be the first nonscientist in space, McAuliffe was selected. In her application she proposed keeping a three-part journal of her experiences: the first part describing the training she would go through, the second chronicling the details of the actual flight, and the third relating her feelings and experiences back on Earth. She also planned to keep a video record of her activities. McAuliffe was to conduct at least two lessons while onboard the space shuttle to be simulcast to students around the world, and she was to spend the nine months following her return home lecturing to students across the United States.

Christa McAuliffe, 1985. NASA

Problems dogged the ill-fated *Challenger* mission from the start: the launch had been postponed for several days, and the night before the launch, central Florida was hit by a severe cold front that left ice on the launchpad. The shuttle finally was launched at 11:38 AM on January 28, 1986. Just 73 seconds after liftoff the craft exploded, sending debris cascading into the Atlantic Ocean for more than an hour afterward. There were no survivors. The live television coverage of the spectacular and tragic event, coupled with McAuliffe's winning, dynamic, and (not least) civilian presence onboard, halted shuttle missions for two and a half years, sorely damaged the reputation of NASA, and eroded public support for the space program.

SIR RICHARD BRANSON

(b. July 18, 1950, Shamley Green, Surrey, England)

The British entrepreneur and adventurer Sir Richard Branson founded Virgin Group Ltd. and became known for his publicity stunts as well as for setting records in powerboat racing and hot-air ballooning.

Branson, who was a school dropout, entered into his first successful business venture as a teenager with the magazine *Student*. When the magazine began losing money in the late 1960s, he formed Virgin Mail Order Records (so named because Branson considered himself inexperienced in business) to raise funds, and in 1971 he opened the first British discount record store. In 1973 he helped form Virgin Records, which quickly became the principal label worldwide for punk and new wave. In 1984 he became the majority backer of the airline that he renamed Virgin Atlantic Airways. Beginning with a single aircraft, the carrier succeeded despite fierce opposition from established airlines, and in 1992 Branson sold Virgin Records to raise additional money for Virgin Atlantic. By the 1990s the Virgin conglomerate, which was among the largest privately held companies in the United Kingdom, comprised some 100 businesses, including Virgin Megastores. In 2004 Branson formed Virgin Galactic, a space tourism company that was working toward offering commercial suborbital passenger flights. In 2006 Branson sold Virgin Mobile, a wireless phone service, though he remained the largest share-holder of the company, which was later renamed Virgin Media, Inc. That same year he formed the collaborative entertainment companies Virgin Comics LLC and Virgin Animation Private Limited.

In 1986 Branson was part of a two-man team that set a record for a powerboat crossing of the Atlantic Ocean. In 1987 he and Swedish aeronaut Per Lindstrand became the first team to cross the Atlantic in a hot-air balloon, and in 1991 the pair became the first to cross the Pacific Ocean. Branson was also a member of teams that made three failed attempts in the late 1990s at round-the-world balloon flights. On the third attempt, in December 1998, the pair were joined by American adventurer Steve Fossett, and they traveled some 8,200 miles (13,200 km), becoming the first to fly across the whole of Asia in a hot-air balloon, before being forced down off Hawaii. Branson later helped fund Fossett's record-setting flight in 2005, in which he completed the first solo, nonstop circumnavigation of the world in an airplane.

Branson's numerous charitable initiatives included pledging an estimated $3 billion in 2006 to fund environmentally friendly fuel research. In 2007, in honour of his sustained support of humanitarian and environmental causes, Branson received the Citizen of the Year Award from the United Nations Correspondents Association (UNCA). He published an autobiography, *Losing My Virginity: How I've Survived, Had Fun, and Made a Fortune Doing Business My Way* (1998, updated ed. 2011). He was knighted in 1999.

MUHAMMED FARIS

(b. May 26, 1951, Aleppo, Syria)

Syrian pilot and air force officer Muhammed Ahmed Faris became, in 1987, the first Syrian citizen to go into space.

After graduating from military pilot school at the Syrian air force academy near Aleppo in 1973, Faris joined the air force and eventually attained the rank of colonel. He also served as an aviation instructor and a specialist in navigation later in his military career. In 1985 he was chosen as one of two Syrian candidates to participate in the Intercosmos spaceflight program, which allowed cosmonauts from allied countries to participate in Soviet space missions. Faris reported to the cosmonaut training centre in Star City, Russia, for training on September 30, 1985.

Faris flew into space as a research cosmonaut on board the Soyuz TM-3 spacecraft on July 22, 1987, as part of the first visiting crew to the Mir orbital space station. The three-man crew included, along with Faris, two Soviet cosmonauts, Aleksandr Viktorenko and Aleksandr P. Aleksandrov. During the mission, Faris conducted several research experiments with his fellow cosmonauts in the fields of space medicine and materials processing. He returned to Earth aboard Soyuz TM-2 on July 30, 1987, having spent a total of eight days in space.

After his mission, Faris returned to the Syrian air force and settled in Aleppo. For his accomplishments as a cosmonaut, he was awarded the title Hero of the Soviet Union, and he also received the Order of Lenin, the Soviet Union's highest civilian decoration.

SALLY RIDE

(b. May 26, 1951, Encino, California, U.S.—
d. July 23, 2012, La Jolla, California),

American astronaut Sally Kristen Ride was the first American woman to travel into outer space. Only two other women preceded her: Valentina Tereshkova (1963) and Svetlana Savitskaya (1982), both from the former Soviet Union.

Ride showed great early promise as a tennis player, but she eventually gave up her plans to play professionally and attended Stanford University, where she earned bachelor's degrees in English and physics (1973). In 1978, as a doctoral candidate and teaching assistant in laser physics at Stanford, she was selected by NASA as one of six women astronaut candidates. She received a Ph.D. in astrophysics and began her training and evaluation courses that same year. In August 1979 she completed her NASA training, obtained a pilot's license, and became eligible for assignment as a U.S. space shuttle mission specialist. On June 18, 1983, she became the first American woman in space while rocketing into orbit aboard the shuttle orbiter *Challenger*. The shuttle mission lasted six days, during which time she helped deploy two communications satellites and carry out a variety of experiments.

Ride served on a second space mission aboard *Challenger* in October 1984; the crew included another woman, Ride's childhood friend Kathryn Sullivan, who became the first American woman to walk in space. Ride was training for a third shuttle mission when the *Challenger* exploded after launch in January 1986, a catastrophe that caused NASA to suspend shuttle flights for more than two years. Ride served on the presidential commission appointed to investigate the accident, and she repeated that role as a member of the commission that investigated the in-flight breakup of the orbiter *Columbia* in February 2003.

Sally Ride serving as mission specialist on the flight deck of the space shuttle orbiter Challenger. NASA

Ride married fellow astronaut Steven Hawley in 1982; they divorced five years later. Ride resigned from NASA in 1987, and in 1989 she became a professor of physics at the University of California, San Diego, and director of its California Space Institute (until 1996). In 1999–2000 she held executive positions with Space.com, a Web site presenting space, astronomy, and technology content. From the 1990s Ride initiated or headed a number of programs and organizations devoted to fostering science in education, particularly to providing support for schoolgirls interested in science, mathematics, or technology. She also wrote or collaborated on several children's books about space exploration and her personal experiences as an astronaut.

JAMES CAMERON

(b. August 16, 1954, Kapuskasing, Ontario, Canada)

The Canadian filmmaker and adventurer James Cameron is best known for his expansive vision and innovative special-effects films, most notably *Titanic* (1997), for which he won an Academy Award for best director, and *Avatar* (2009). He is also noted for his undersea exploration in submersible watercraft.

Cameron studied art as a child; he later provided the drawings that figured prominently in *Titanic*. In 1971 his family moved to California. After studying physics at California State University at Fullerton, Cameron worked at a series of jobs, including machinist and truck driver, before a viewing of *Star Wars* (1977) inspired him to try his hand at moviemaking.

In 1980 Cameron was hired as a production designer, and the following year he made his directorial debut with *Piranha II: The Spawning*. A flop at the box office, the movie encouraged Cameron to write his own material. The result was *Terminator* (1984), an action thriller about a robot hit man that made actor Arnold Schwarzenegger a star and established Cameron as a bankable filmmaker. A series of high-tech and big-budget pictures followed, including *Aliens* (1986) and *The Abyss* (1989), each of which received an Oscar for best visual effects, *Terminator 2: Judgment Day* (1991), and *True Lies* (1994). In 1992 Cameron formed his own production company, Lightstorm Entertainment, and the following year he cofounded Digital Domain, a state-of-the-art effects company.

Although his films met with success at the box office, many viewers complained that the films lacked substance and relied too heavily on visual effects. In 1998 Cameron defied critics with *Titanic*, his screen adaptation of the doomed ocean liner's 1912 maiden voyage. Written, directed, and coproduced by Cameron, *Titanic* was one of the most expensive movies ever made, but it broke box-office records and tied *Ben-Hur* (1959) for most Academy Awards won (11). Skillfully blending special effects with a fictional love story between a penniless artist (played by American actor Leonardo DiCaprio) and an unhappily engaged first-class passenger (British actress Kate Winslet), *Titanic* stood atop the American charts for an unprecedented 15 weeks and earned more than $1.8 billion to become the highest-grossing movie in the world.

Following *Titanic*'s unparalleled success, Cameron took a break from feature films. He created and coproduced *Dark Angel* (2000–01), a science-fiction television

(From left) *Kate Winslet, Leonardo DiCaprio, and James Cameron on the set of the film* Titanic *(1997).* Courtesy of Twentieth Century-Fox Film Corporation

series about a genetically altered female warrior, and he made several documentaries. *Expedition: Bismarck* (2002) took the director and his crew deep into the Atlantic Ocean, where they captured footage of the sunken Nazi battleship *Bismarck*. The documentary won an Emmy Award. Other underwater excursions were chronicled in *Ghosts of the Abyss* (2003), which explored the *Titanic*, and *Aliens of the Deep* (2005).

In 2009 Cameron returned to feature films with *Avatar*, a science-fiction thriller that was noted for its special effects. A major box-office success, it surpassed *Titanic* to become the highest-grossing movie in the world, earning more than $2.5 billion. The movie also received critical acclaim. At the Golden Globes ceremony in 2010,

Cameron received the award for best director, and the film was named best picture.

Cameron remained involved in underwater exploration, and in 2012 he debuted the *Deepsea Challenger*, a submersible that he codesigned. Described as a "vertical torpedo," the one-person vehicle performed quick ascents and descents and was able to withstand extreme pressure. In March Cameron completed a test dive in which he traveled to a depth of approximately 5 miles (8 km), a record for a solo mission. Later that month he journeyed nearly 7 miles (11 km) below the Pacific Ocean to explore the Challenger Deep, the world's deepest known recess, in the Mariana Trench.

ANN BANCROFT

(b. September 29, 1955, St. Paul, Minnesota, U.S.)

The American explorer Ann Bancroft was the first woman to participate in and successfully finish several arduous expeditions to the Arctic and Antarctic.

She grew up in rural Minnesota in what she described as a family of risk takers. Although she struggled with a learning disability, she graduated from St. Paul Academy and Summit School and became a physical education teacher, coach, and wilderness instructor in the Saint Paul area.

When an opportunity arose to participate in the 1986 Steger International Polar Expedition, Bancroft resigned her teaching position. The group departed from Ellesmere Island on March 6, and after 56 days she and five other team members arrived at the North Pole by dogsled without benefit of resupply. She thus became the first woman to reach the North Pole by sled and on foot. In 1992 she also was the leader of the first team of women to ski across Greenland. In November 1992 she led three other women on the grassroots-funded American Women's Expedition to Antarctica. By successfully completing their 67-day, 660-mile (1,060-km) journey in early 1993, they became the first women's team to reach the South Pole on skis, and Bancroft was the first woman to have stood at both poles. Bancroft returned to Antarctica in 2001, when she and Norwegian polar explorer Liv Arensen became the first women to complete a transcontinental crossing there. Their roughly 1,700-mile (2,750-km) journey skiing and sailing took 94 days. In recognition of her achievements, she was inducted into the National Women's Hall of Fame in 1995, and she received several additional awards and honours.

SALMĀN ĀL SAʻŪD

(b. June 27, 1956, Riyadh, Saudi Arabia)

In 1985 Prince Sultān ibn Salmān ibn ʻAbd al-ʻAzīz Āl Saʻūd became the first Saudi Arabian citizen, the first Arab, the first Muslim, and the first member of a royal family to travel into space.

Educated in the United States, Salmān received a degree in mass communications from the University of Denver (Colorado) and earned a master's degree in social and political science from the Maxwell School of Citizenship and Public Affairs at Syracuse University (New York). He later worked at the Ministry of Information in Saudi Arabia as a researcher and served as the deputy director for the Saudi Arabian Olympic Information Committee at the 1984 Olympic Games in Los Angeles. In 1985 he was commissioned as an officer in the Royal Saudi Air Force and served as a fighter pilot. He retired from military service with the rank of colonel.

Later that year Salmān was chosen by NASA as a payload specialist for the STS-51G space shuttle mission. He embarked on an abbreviated training schedule, and on June 17, 1985, Salmān flew on the space shuttle *Discovery* as part of a seven-member international crew. During the seven-day mission, Salmān represented the Arab Satellite Communications Organization (ARABSAT) and took part in the deployment of the organization's satellite, ARABSAT-1B. While in space, he also carried out a series of experiments that had been designed by Saudi scientists, including an ionized gas experiment set up by another member of the Saudi royal family for his Ph.D. dissertation and an experiment concerning the behaviour of oil and water when mixed in zero gravity. Salmān also spoke to his uncle, King Fahd, by telephone while in space and conducted a guided tour of the space shuttle's interior in Arabic, which was broadcast on television channels in the Middle East. The shuttle landed back on Earth on June 24, 1985.

Upon his return, Salmān became a founding member of the Association of Space Explorers, an international organization for astronauts and cosmonauts who have traveled into space, and served on its board of directors. His unique accomplishments brought him numerous state honours, particularly from Muslim and Arab countries such as Pakistan, Kuwait, Qatar, Bahrain, Morocco, and Syria.

Salmān was appointed as the first secretary-general of the Supreme Tourism Commission in Saudi Arabia when the organization was formed in 2000. In this position, he worked to expand and enhance the tourism sector in his country by playing a leading role in developing the country's tourism strategy and devising the industry's regulations. He remained as head of the organization when, in 2008, its name was changed to the Saudi Commission for Tourism and Antiquities.

Mae Jemison

(b. October 17, 1956, Decatur, Alabama, U.S.)

M ae Carol Jemison, an American physician and the first African American woman to become an astronaut, spent more than a week orbiting Earth in the space shuttle *Endeavour* in 1992.

Jemison moved with her family to Chicago at the age of three. There she was introduced to science by her uncle and developed interests throughout her childhood in anthropology, archaeology, evolution, and astronomy. While still a high school student, she became interested in biomedical engineering, and after graduating in 1973,

Mae Jemison aboard the space shuttle Endeavour. NASA Marshall Space Flight Center

at the age of 16, she entered Stanford University. There she received degrees in chemical engineering and African American studies (1977).

In 1977 Jemison entered medical school at Cornell University in Ithaca, New York, where she pursued an interest in international medicine. After volunteering for a summer in a Cambodian refugee camp in Thailand, she studied in Kenya in 1979. She graduated from medical school in 1981, and, after a short time as a general practitioner with a Los Angeles medical group, she became a medical officer with the Peace Corps in West Africa. There she managed health care for Peace Corps and U.S. embassy personnel and worked in conjunction with the National Institutes of Health and the Centers for Disease Control on several research projects, including development of a hepatitis B vaccine.

After returning to the United States, Jemison applied to NASA to be an astronaut. In October 1986, she was among 15 people accepted out of 2,000 applicants. Jemison completed her training as a mission specialist with NASA in 1988. She became an astronaut office representative with the Kennedy Space Center at Cape Canaveral, Florida, working to process space shuttles for launching and to verify shuttle software. Next, she was assigned to support a cooperative mission between the United States and Japan designed to conduct experiments in materials processing and the life sciences. In September 1992, STS-47 Spacelab J became the first successful joint U.S.-Japan space mission.

Jemison's maiden space flight came with the week-long September 1992 mission of the shuttle *Endeavour*. At that time she was the only African American woman astronaut. After completing her NASA mission, she formed the Jemison Group, to develop and market advanced technologies. She was inducted into the National Women's Hall of Fame in 1993.

BERTRAND PICCARD

(b. March 1, 1958, Lausanne, Switzerland)

On March 20, 1999, with copilot Brian Jones, the Swiss aviator and adventurer Bertrand Piccard completed the first nonstop circumnavigation of Earth by balloon. The trip, begun by Piccard and Jones on March 1 aboard the *Breitling Orbiter 3*, took 19 days, 21 hours, and 55 minutes to complete. Starting in the Swiss Alps, the balloon carried the pair over Europe, Africa, Asia, Central America, and the Pacific and Atlantic oceans.

Piccard, the captain of the *Breitling Orbiter 3*, was the grandson of Auguste Piccard, who was the first person to reach the stratosphere by balloon, and the son of Jacques Piccard, who designed and piloted bathyscaphes for deep-sea exploration. He became an expert hang-gliding pilot as a child and later piloted ultralight planes and hot-air balloons. Although he trained as a psychiatrist and established a practice in Lausanne, he continued to devote a large part of his time to ballooning. In 1992 Piccard and Wim Verstraeten crossed the Atlantic Ocean, winning the Chrysler Transatlantic Challenge. The pair made two unsuccessful attempts to circle the globe: the first, in 1997, ended with a fuel leak that released toxic fumes into their cabin; and the second try, a 1998 flight in the *Breitling Orbiter 2*, ended in a rice paddy in Myanmar (Burma).

In the months leading up to Piccard and Jones's triumphant flight, several prominent individuals, including

Bertrand Piccard, 1999.
Breitling SA

British billionaire Richard Branson and American adventurer Steve Fossett, failed in their attempts to circumnavigate the globe via balloon. Piccard and Jones were forced to bypass a number of no-fly zones, but they were granted permission to fly over southern China and thus were able to ride a crucial jet stream air flow over the Pacific Ocean. Their historic flight concluded with a safe landing near the Pyramids of Giza, in Egypt, on March 21. The *Breitling Orbiter 3* gondola subsequently was placed on display at the Smithsonian Institution's National Air and Space Museum in Washington, D.C. Piccard was awarded the Legion of Honour by the French government in 2001.

After completing the around-the-world trip with Jones, Piccard used his fame to further a number of philanthropic endeavours. In 2003, with Swiss engineer and pilot André Borschberg, Piccard launched Solar Impulse, a project that had the ultimate goal of developing and launching a solar-powered airplane capable of circumnavigating the globe. The first of those planes, Solar Impulse HB-SIA, was completed in 2009, and a major step was achieved when the plane, piloted by Borschberg, completed a 26-hour flight over Switzerland on July 7–8, 2010, becoming the first solar-powered aircraft to fly through the night. Other pioneering milestones included an international flight from Payern, Switzerland, to Brussels, Belgium in May 2011 and, in June, from Brussels to Paris; and a 19-hour transcontinental flight from Madrid, Spain, to Rabat, Morocco, in 2012. Construction began in 2011 on the larger Solar Impulse HB-SIB, intended for use in the round-the-world flight attempt.

APA SHERPA

(b. c. 1960, Thami, Nepal)

The Nepali mountaineer and guide Apa (or Appa) Sherpa—in full, Lhakpa Tenzing Sherpa—is best known for having achieved the most ascents of Mount Everest.

Apa was raised in the small village of Thami (or Thame) in the Khumbu valley of far northern Nepal, just west of Mount Everest. The area is well known for its Sherpas (ethnic Nepalis, Tibetans, and Sikkimese who serve as porters and guides on expeditions in the Himalayas), including famed climber Tenzing Norgay, who once lived in Thami. Apa's family, like most in the region, was extremely poor. His father was a herdsman who died when Apa was about 12 years old. Apa, being the oldest child, left school and began carrying supplies for trekking parties in the area to help support his family. He quickly impressed his employers with his ability to haul large loads (despite his small size) and his cheerful disposition. One of his European patrons sponsored his enrollment at the

Himalayan Trust School (established by Everest climbing pioneer Sir Edmund Hillary) in Khumjung, near Thami. However, the family's circumstances forced Apa to leave school after a couple of years and return to his porter job.

In 1985 he joined his first major mountaineering expedition, to Annapurna, where he worked as a cook, and he returned to that mountain as a porter in 1987. Apa began working on Everest trips in 1988, participating in several unsuccessful summit attempts over the next two years. He finally reached the top in May 1990, when he joined a New Zealand expedition with other first-time summiters Peter Hillary (son of Sir Edmund) and Rob Hall (who became a leader of expeditions on Everest, including an ill-fated trip in 1996).

For more than two decades thereafter, Apa embarked on an almost unbroken string of annual ascents up Everest that included two successful climbs in 1992. In only two years did he not reach the summit: in 1996, when he made no climbs, and in 2001, when the attempt was abandoned because of bad weather. In 2000, with his 11th trip to the top, he broke the record for the most Everest summits, and he then established a new record with each successive climb.

Apa joined the first Eco Everest Expedition in 2008 and participated in subsequent years. Each of these trips, in addition to a summit climb, focused on publicizing ecological and climate-change issues affecting Everest—notably, the accelerated melting of the giant Khumbu Icefall near the mountain's base. The expeditions employed ecologically friendly practices (e.g., the use of solar cookers) and collected and took down tons of trash and camping and climbing gear left behind by earlier expeditions. Apa's climb in May 2010 was especially notable because it was his 20th successful Everest ascent. A year later, in May 2011, he completed his 21st summit. Later that year he announced his retirement from high-altitude climbing, but he stayed active in the Himalayas. In January–April 2012 he participated in a 99-day trek through that range to publicize concerns about climate change in the region.

In 2006 Apa and his family moved to the United States to give his children educational opportunities that he had missed. However, he still wished to help his native Thami, and in 2010 he established the Apa Sherpa Foundation to further educational and economic opportunities there and elsewhere in the region.

GERLINDE KALTENBRUNNER

(b. December 13, 1970, Kirchdorf an der Krems?, Austria)

The Austrian mountain climber Gerlinde Kaltenbrunner became one of the first women to climb all 14 of the world's peaks 26,250 feet (8,000 metres) and higher and the first woman to do so without using supplemental oxygen-breathing apparatus.

Kaltenbrunner grew up in the small resort community of Spital am Pyhrn, nestled in the Alps of central Austria. As a child, she became an accomplished skier, but she gradually became more interested in trekking in the mountains near her home. Her first climbing expedition was at the age of 13, when she ascended Sturzhahn (6,654 feet [2,028 metres]), a mountain in west-central Austria. Kaltenbrunner continued improving her mountaineering skills in the Alps during her adolescence and while she pursued training as a nurse. In addition, after seeing photographs of the high mountains of the Karakoram Range (stretching along the portions of the Kashmir region administered by Pakistan, China, and India) when she was 16, she resolved to someday climb 26,250-foot (8,000-metre) peaks in south-central Asia.

Kaltenbrunner ascended the first of these mountains, Broad Peak in the Karakorams, in 1994, although she reached a lower peak (26,335 feet [8,027 metres]) than the true summit. Over the next 17 years she climbed to the top of all 14 giants, beginning with Cho Oyu (26,906 feet [8,201 metres]) in the central Himalayas near Mount Everest in 1998. She employed the Alpine style of mountaineering pioneered by climber Reinhold Messner and others, in which climbers carry a minimal amount of equipment on expeditions, have little or no outside support (e.g., porters), and do not use supplemental oxygen. This style is particularly challenging for people climbing at elevations above 26,250 feet (8,000 metres), the benchmark for a region known as the "death zone" for the thinness of the air there.

At first Kaltenbrunner's nursing work financed her expeditions, but, after successfully scaling Nanga Parbat (26,660 feet [8,126 metres]) in the western Himalayas in 2003, she became a full-time professional climber. Whereas it had taken her nearly a decade to reach the tops of her first four 26,250-foot (8,000-metre) peaks, she was able to climb all of the remaining ones in the next eight years, scaling two each in 2004 and 2005. This included reascending Broad Peak to its true summit (26,401 feet [8,047 metres]) in 2007 and also Xixabangma (26,286 feet [8,012 metres]) in 2005, which, in 2000, she also had climbed to a lower summit. Several of those mountains involved more than one attempt to reach the top, among them Mount Everest (29,035 feet [8,850 metres]), the world's tallest mountain, where she was unsuccessful in 2005 but prevailed in 2010; and K2 (28,251 feet [8,611 metres]) in the Karakorams, the world's second highest peak, which took several aborted tries (notably in 2007, 2009, and 2010) before she finally reached the summit of this her last 26,250-foot (8,000-metre) peak in August 2011.

During the time that Kaltenbrunner was seeking her goal, two other climbers—Oh Eun-Sun of South Korea and Edurne Pasaban of Spain—were also on track to become the first woman to summit all of the 14. Kaltenbrunner maintained that she was not competing with them and even climbed two of the peaks, Broad in 2007 and Dhaulagiri I (26,795 feet [8,167 metres]; in Nepal) in 2008, at the same time as Pasaban. Oh topped her final peak, Annapurna I (26,545 feet [8,091 metres]), also in Nepal, in April 2010, but controversy arose regarding the veracity of her claimed 2009 summit of Kanchenjunga (28,169 feet [8,586 metres]) on the India-Nepal border. Pasaban indisputably topped her 14th peak, Xixabangma, in May 2010, climbing each except for Everest without supplemental oxygen. Thus, when Kaltenbrunner completed her K2 climb, she became the first woman to summit all 14 without oxygen. Kaltenbrunner was married to German mountaineer Ralf Dujmovits, who accompanied her on several expeditions and who also had climbed all 14 of the 26,250-foot (8,000-metre) peaks.

CONCLUSION

The 20th century produced a dizzying number of extraordinary explorers and, increasingly, adventurers who penetrated virtually every remaining corner of Earth yet to be visited. Much of their focus was thus on the most remote and environmentally extreme locales. The polar regions were the major emphasis during the first half of the century, with both poles being definitively reached by the mid-1920s. Although the polar regions remained of great interest to scientists and adventurers well into the 21st century, many after World War II also set their sights on conquering the tallest mountains, the greatest heights of the atmosphere, and the farthest depths of the oceans. Sir Edmund Hillary and Tenzing Norgay climbed to the top of Mount Everest—Earth's highest point—in 1953, and members of the remarkable Piccard family managed to reach the upper limit of the atmosphere and the deepest part of the ocean in crafts that they had helped to design and build.

The great remaining quest for the century was space, the "final" frontier. Aerospace technology advanced rapidly after World War II with the development of first jet and then rocket propulsion. In the 1950s experimental aircraft reached for the upper limits of the atmosphere and even ventured into space before rocketry was perfected enough to actually allow people to travel there. The first humans reached space in the early 1960s, and by the end of the decade the United States had put men on the Moon. As extraordinary a technological feat as this was, it also required great courage and skill on the part of those who journeyed there. Although the lunar program was abandoned in the early 1970s after only six Moon landings, men and women remained in space aboard a series of space stations in orbit around Earth. The most recent of these stations was the International Space Station, the first portion of which became operational in 1998.

In the latter part of the 20th century and certainly by the start of the 21st, exploration on Earth in many ways was gradually giving way to adventurism. It was not enough for Reinhold Messner to climb Everest; he had to attempt it, as well as all of the other peaks above 26,250 feet (8,000 metres), without supplemental oxygen. Once Charles Lindbergh had made his pioneering transatlantic flight in 1927, others followed across that ocean in balloons, planes, motorboats, and one-person sailboats.

Great advances in technology made it increasingly possible for growing numbers of people to attempt these ventures. Since the 1980s, hundreds of climbers have attempted to scale Everest and other tall peaks each year, many of them have succeeded. Countless others strike out on other adventures—skiing across Antarctica, flying solo around the world without landing, and various other extraordinary endeavours that test the limits of human endurance and ingenuity.

GLOSSARY

aeronautics A science dealing with the operation of aircraft.

antiquities Matters and items relating to the life or culture of ancient times.

ascent The act of rising or climbing upward by degrees.

ballast A heavy substance placed in such a way as to improve stability and control of a vessel, particularly ships and passenger balloons.

bathyscaphe A navigable submersible craft for deep-sea exploration having a spherical watertight cabin attached to its underside.

circumnavigate To travel completely around the world.

conquistador One who conquers; particularly a Spanish leader of the 16th century.

dirigible Another name for an airship, such as a balloon.

ethnologist A practitioner of the anthropological sciences, who studies human culture based on ethnicity and other factors.

expedition A journey or excursion undertaken for a specific purpose.

funerary Of or pertaining to burials.

hominin Any of a taxonomic tribe of primates that includes recent humans, together with extinct ancestral and related forms.

naturalist A student of natural history; a field biologist.

poacher One who kills or takes wild game or fish illegally.

reconnoitre To engage in reconnaissance; to survey an area in order to gather information.

sherpa A member of a Tibetan people of eastern Nepal known for providing support for foreign trekkers and mountain climbers.

sledge A strong, heavy sled used for traveling over rough, frigid terrain.

subversion The act of undermining, overthrowing, or corrupting.

summit The highest point, particularly in regard to mountain peaks.

topography The configuration of a surface including its relief and the position of its natural and man-made features.

transit The act of passing through or over; in astronomy, the passage of a smaller body across the disk of a larger body.

whet To make sharper, keener, or more aware.

BIBLIOGRAPHY

A comprehensive overview is Raymond John Howgego, *Encyclopedia of Exploration*, vols. 3 & 4 (2006–08), which details late 19th- and early 20th-century exploration and travel.

Farley Mowat, *Ordeal by Ice* (1961), *The Polar Passion* (1967), and *Tundra* (1973), also published together as *The Top of the World*, 3 vol. (1973, reprinted 1989), provide an excellent summary of and introduction to the history of exploration of the Canadian Arctic, with lengthy excerpts from firsthand accounts; and Wally Herbert, *The Noose of Laurels: The Discovery of the North Pole* (1989), is an expert analysis of the probability of either Cook or Peary having reached the North Pole. Roald Amundsen, *The Amundsen Photographs*, ed. by Roland Huntford (1987), offers visual imagery to accompany the other accounts of the Arctic explorations. Raimund E. Goerler (ed.), *To the Pole: The Diary and Notebook of Richard E. Byrd*, 1925–1927 (1998), is Byrd's handwritten account of his North Pole flight; and Simon Nasht, *The Last Explorer: Hubert Wilkins, Hero of the Great Age of Polar Exploration* (also published as The *Last Explorer: Hubert Wilkins, Australia's Unknown Hero*, 2005), is a useful biography of the polar aviator.

Antarctica: Great Stories from the Frozen Continent, 1st rev. ed. (1988), published by *Reader's Digest*, offers a readable and profusely illustrated account; Roland Huntford, *Scott and Amundsen* (1979, reissued 1993; also published as *The Last Place on Earth*, 1984), critically examines Robert Falcon Scott's planning, judgment, and leadership on his fatal Antarctic expedition; and G.E. Fogg, *A History of*

Antarctic Science (1992, reprinted 2005), traces the development of scientific inquiry in Antarctica.

Günter Oskar Dyhrenfurth, *To the Third Pole: The History of the High Himalaya* (1955, reissued 1994), is a general history of climbing in the Himalayas. Works on the exploration and climbing of Mount Everest include Walt Unsworth, *Everest* (1981, 3rd rev. ed., 2000); Leni Gillman and Peter Gillman, *Everest: Eighty Years of Triumph and Tragedy* (1993, rev. ed. 2001); and The Royal Geographical Society, *Everest: Summit of Achievement* (2003). Edmund Hillary, *The View From the Summit* (1999, reissued 2003), is the autobiography of the famous conqueror of Everest; and Ed Douglas, *Tenzing: Hero of Everest* (2003), is a sensitive biography of Hillary's partner.

Doris L. Rich, *Queen Bess: Daredevil Aviator* (1993); and Elizabeth Amelia Hadley Freydberg, *Bessie Coleman: The Brownskin Lady Bird* (1994), cover Coleman's life and career. Biographies of Charles Lindbergh include Walter S. Ross, *The Last Hero: Charles A. Lindbergh*, rev. ed. (1976, reissued 2005); Brendan Gill, *Lindbergh Alone* (1977, reissued 2002); and A. Scott Berg, *Lindbergh* (1998). Amelia Earhart's life is the subject of Mary S. Lovell, *The Sound of Wings* (1989); Susan Butler, *East to the Dawn* (1997); and Donald M. Goldstein and Katherine V. Dillon, *Amelia* (1997). Randall Brink, *Lost Star: The Search for Amelia Earhart* (1994), examines her disappearance. Pierre de Latil and Jean Rivoire, *A la recherche du monde marin* (1954; *Man and the Underwater World*, 1956), deals with the explorations undertaken by Auguste and Jacques Piccard.

Biographies of T.E. Lawrence include Robert Graves, *Lawrence and the Arabs* (1927, reissued 1991), a book vetted by Lawrence; Jean Béraud-Villars, T.E. Lawrence; or, *The Search for the Absolute* (1959), one of the best studies of the man; and Jeremy Wilson, *Lawrence of Arabia: The Authorised Biography of T.E. Lawrence* (1989). An account of Howard Carter's excavation of Tutankhamen's tomb is *C.W. Ceram, Gods, Graves & Scholars* (2nd rev. and enlarged ed., 1994). Farley Mowat, *Woman in the Mists: The Story of Dian Fossey and the Mountain Gorillas of Africa* (1987, reissued 1994), looks at her life and work.

Broad coverage of space activities can be found in Fernand Verger, Isabelle Sourbès-Verger, and Raymond Ghirardi, *The Cambridge Encyclopedia of Space: Missions, Applications, and Exploration* (2003). An overall history of space exploration is William E. Burrows, *This New Ocean: The Story of the First Space Age* (1998). An account of the Apollo program that is focused on the astronauts is Andrew Chaikin, *A Man on the Moon: The Voyages of the Apollo Astronauts* (1994, reissued in 3 vol., 1999). Boris E. Chertok, *Rockets and People*, 4 vol. (2004–11), offers fascinating insights into the development of the Soviet space program by a former Soviet aerospace engineer. *Virgil I. Grissom, 1964.* NASA

INDEX